The Small Book of Big Presentation Skills

Also from Lexden Publishing:

Title	Author	ISBN
Computer Systems Architecture	R Newman, E Gaura, D Hibbs	1-903337-07-0
Computer Networks (2nd Edition)	P Irving	1-904995-08-X
Databases	R Warrender	1-903337-08-9
JavaScript: Creating Dynamic Web Pages	E Gandy, S Stobart	1-904995-07-1
Multimedia Computing	D Cunliffe, G Elliott	1-904995-05-5
User Interface Design	J Le Peuple, R Scane	1-903337-19-4
Visual Programming	D Leigh	1-903337-11-9
Access 2002: An Advanced Course for Students	S Coles, J Rowley	1-904995-06-3
Access 2000: An Introductory Course for Students	S Coles, J Rowley	1-903300-14-2
Access 2000: An Advanced Course for Students	S Coles, J Rowley	1-903300-15-0
Excel 2000: An Introductory Course for Students	J Muir	1-903300-16-9
Excel 2000: An Advanced Course for Students	J Muir	1-903300-16-9
Excel 2002: An Advanced Course for Students	J Muir	1-84445-005-8
Word 2000: An Introductory Course for Students	S Coles, J Rowley	1-903300-18-5
Word 2000: An Advanced Course for Students	S Coles, J Rowley	1-903300-19-3
Key Skills Level 1: Communication; Application of Number; Information and Communication Technology	R Whitley Willis, L Gabrielle	1-904995-10-1
Key Skills Level 2: Communication; Application of Number; Information and Communication Technology	R Whitley Willis, L Gabrielle	1-904995-17-9

The Small Book of Big Presentation Skills

Rajeev K Bali
and
Ashish Dwivedi

Lexden Publishing
www.lexden-publishing.co.uk

For our families

First published in 2006 by Lexden Publishing Ltd.

British Library Cataloguing in Publication Data
A CIP record for this book is available from the British Library.
ISBN-10: 1 904995 17 9
ISBN-13: 978 1 904995 17 3

Printed by Lightning Source

Lexden Publishing Ltd
23 Irvine Road
Colchester
Essex
C03 3TS

Tel: 01206 533164
Email: info@lexden-publishing.co.uk
www.lexden-publishing.co.uk

"We had snakes in Raiders of the Lost Ark
and bugs in Indiana Jones and the Temple of Doom,
but supposedly man's greatest fear is public speaking.
That'll be in our next picture."

STEVEN SPIELBERG

CONTENTS

Acknowledgements

One of our many intentions for this book was to include comments and anecdotes from both students and academics. From these, we trust that you can gain a valuable insight into the typical thoughts of both your peers and your target audience (academics).

We are therefore indebted to the following academic colleagues for their contributions: Dr Chris Bloor (University of Sunderland), Professor Brian Lehaney (Coventry University) and Dr Gerry Urwin (Coventry University).

We further thank the following former undergraduate and postgraduate students for their insights: Laura Harrison, Ameneh Mojtabai, Jonathan Murphy, Paris Parissis, Alex Saunders and Tim Thompson.

We acknowledge the use of many quotes, quips and anecdotes from politicians, comedians, stars of the silver screen and TV, authors and raconteurs; either by intention or accident, these quotes were often deep in meaning and high in mirth.

Special thanks to Jonathan Lynn and Antony Jay for their kind permission to reproduce lines from "Yes, Prime Minister".

Our thanks to Mark Kench at Lexden Publishing for green-lighting the project, his patient assistance and helpful comments.

We acknowledge that Microsoft, Windows and PowerPoint are either registered trademarks or trademarks of Microsoft Corporation in the United States and/or other countries. Microsoft product screen shot(s) reprinted with permission from Microsoft Corporation. "The Small Book of Big Presentation Skills" is an independent book and is not affiliated with, nor has it been authorised, sponsored, or otherwise approved by Microsoft Corporation.

Last, but by no means least, we thank our respective families for their support during the management of this, our latest project.

Rajeev K Bali, PhD
Warwickshire, UK
r.bali@ieee.org

Ashish Dwivedi, PhD
Hull, UK
A.Dwivedi@hull.ac.uk

About the authors

RAJEEV K BALI BSc(Hons) MSc PhD PgC SMIEEE is a Reader in Healthcare Knowledge Management, Faculty of Engineering and Computing at Coventry University (UK). He is an invited contributor and reviewer for various international journals and conferences. His main research interests are clinical knowledge management and personal and professional development. He has taught presentation skills for several years to both undergraduate and postgraduate students. Previously, he trained local, regional and national organisations in the art of effective business presentations. His involvement with a DTI-funded project afforded him the opportunity to refine these skills further. Previous consultancy work offered him the further opportunity to mentor, coach and facilitate understanding in this key area. He has a biographical entry in *Who's Who in the World.*

ASHISH DWIVEDI BA MBA MSc PhD is a lecturer at Hull University Business School, UK. His primary research interest lies in the application of Information and Communication Technologies (ICT) and Knowledge Management (KM) paradigms on clinical organisational decision-making, on which he completed his PhD. He has taught presentation skills for a number of years both in academic and industrial settings. Collaborative and consultancy work allows him to further disseminate his presentation knowledge and experience.

Preface

As a student, giving a presentation is one of the most nerve-racking and seemingly unrewarding experiences that can be gone through. The very thought of standing in front of tutors (and perhaps even peers) and delivering a speech, however short, turns many peoples' knees to jelly.

In reality though, giving a presentation should be seen as a test, effective passing of which is a necessary skill when you go job-hunting or present at conferences. How many job advertisements have you seen which ask for "excellent presentation skills" or "strong communication skills" or somesuch? If your aim is to land a job in industry, then you will almost certainly be working in a team and, as your experience grows, perhaps one day leading one. With leadership comes the responsibility to nurture and communicate. Knowledge of how to deliver an effective presentation should be seen as a key skill to possess.

After extensive discussions and focus groups with former students, conference and workshop delegates, business managers and leading academics, it is apparent that there is a need for an accessible yet functional text in this area, one that incorporates valuable insights from all stakeholders.

Our own perspective on available texts on presentation skills is that, whilst they are worthy, they promise much but deliver proportionately little. The inclusion of advanced "presentation theory", which although perhaps of interest to other academics, is mainly considered to be superfluous by students who often do not have the time or the inclination to read or digest such information; much of this "extra" knowledge is therefore of little or no relevance to them.

We have come across many texts purporting to teach presentation skills but, in all honesty, could not recommend any to our own students. The aim of this book is to demystify the presentation process and to offer both guidance and advice.

The key aims of this text were to meet the following requirements:

- **genuinely meeting student needs** – it is often the case that texts are designed for managers who have some experience of delivering presentations that requires refinement;
- **relevance** – UK students require a text which, although embedded in theory, gets "to the point" as quickly as possible;
- **offer the UK experience** – students have complained that too many texts deal with American-based scenarios and nuances – if these were to be followed and applied by a UK student, they might result in scorn and disinterest from the proposed audience.

Features

Building on our extensive experience of designing and delivering presentations, it was our intention to produce a text that is at once a useful and accessible guide to essential presentation skills for students. Taking into account student comments about other presentation texts, we have innovatively included comments and observations from students and academics. These intersperse the text in the form of boxes and, by their inclusion, may echo your own questions and concerns.

> *"Speak when you are angry – and you will make the best speech you'll ever regret."*
>
> ***Laurence J Peter (1919 – 1988)***

As presentations (and learning about them) should be fun, we have also included quotes and observations from several famous (and infamous) persons, which provide a terrific insight into the many different facets of presentation skills.

Organisation of the book

We have tried to present the book in as accessible a manner as possible. Following discussions with staff and former students and from our own experiences, we formed a consensus opinion as to the typical thoughts of a student making preparations for a presentation. Which factors to consider, the balance between style and content, how to introduce yourself, how to conclude and how to handle questions were some of the many questions and concerns in the minds of students.

Using this as our guide, we have organised the book in the following manner:

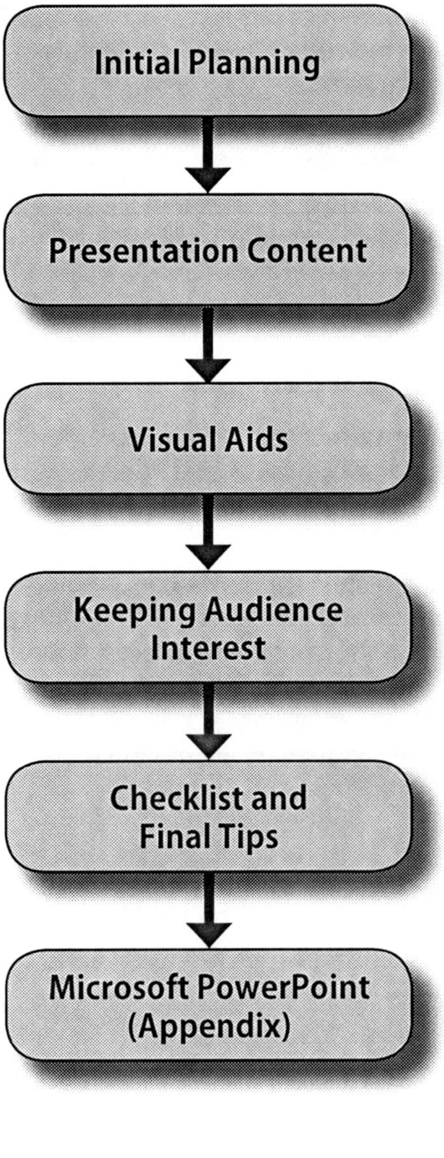

Chapter 1 starts by explaining how best to prepare for and research topics to include in your presentation. Additionally, the chapter allows you to appraise your audience and sets the foundation for the rest of the presentation.

Chapter 2 deals with presentation content. Following on from Chapter 1, this chapter ensures that you not only have enough relevant content for your presentation but that you are also comfortable with it.

Chapter 3 tackles the tricky subject of presentation design. This is perhaps one of the simplest aspects of presentations but one which students get wrong time and time again. One of the key lessons of this chapter is explaining why, at times, less is more.

Chapter 4 explains how, once you have researched content and designed the presentation, you can effectively put these items across to your audience. Keeping your audience interested in your presentation is a delicate balancing act between style and content.

Chapter 5 presents several checklists which you can use as a summary of best practice for your presentation. We end this chapter with anecdotes and vignettes from both former students and staff.

Finally, we have included an appendix on Microsoft® PowerPoint®. This section can be used as either an *aide memoire* or as a quick introduction to the most salient features of this vastly popular presentation tool.

Why not integrate PowerPoint® throughout the book?

We have deliberately chosen not to integrate PowerPoint® examples throughout the text as we feel that this can cause unschooled presenters to rely too much on the technology. As we explain in the text, the presenter should be in charge of the presentation, not the technology.

By not incorporating PowerPoint® examples throughout the text, we have ensured that the central precepts of good presentation techniques and practice are transferred. If you want to use PowerPoint®, then the same precepts can be applied. Our approach is useful for presenters who wish to offer overhead projector (OHP) based presentations (which you may be forced to switch to in case of IT failure – it does happen from time to time!)

And finally...

As you will hear time and time again from your own tutors, the key to success for presentations is patience, practice and the willingness to learn from mistakes – both your own and those made by others. The saying "practice makes perfect" has never been so true...

Chapter 1

INITIAL PLANNING

Chapter summary

This chapter emphasises the need to carry out effective research, which begins well before you begin to plan your presentation design and delivery techniques. We discuss substance, style and delivery and the role of professional behaviour and attitude.

Learning outcomes

After studying this chapter, you should be able to:

Outcome 1: appreciate the importance of good presentation technique.

Outcome 2: assess the value of researching details such as room layout, lighting and pointing.

Outcome 3: recognise the basic concepts of body language.

Planning for presentations

You may have been told, or perhaps are already aware, that an effective presentation is a combination of three essential factors:

- substance;
- style;
- delivery.

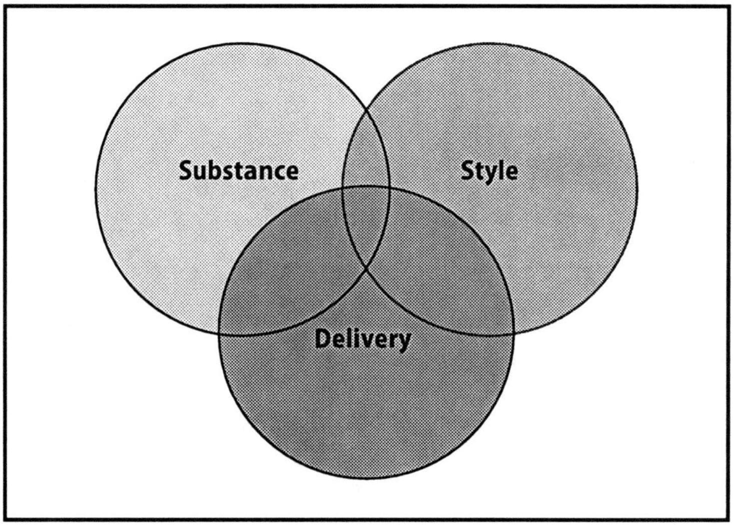

The ideal presentation

Whilst these three factors are crucial to the success of a good presentation, there is an additional aspect, perhaps of even more importance: research.

Research of course is applicable for the substance, style and delivery aspects of presentations, but one must not forget the research that needs to be undertaken before these three aspects are approached.

> *"An original idea. That can't be too hard. The library must be full of them."*
>
> ***Stephen Fry***

Many novice presenters forget this fourth aspect completely, concentrating solely on the most common three. This type of research is background or preparatory in nature and includes the following items:

Researching...the room

If at all possible, try to take a look at your presentation room beforehand. Pay careful attention to the room design, lighting, whether it is too warm or too cold and so forth. By knowing a little of what lies ahead, you can plan accordingly.

Check also to see whether there is electronic projection, a computer, a lectern, a projection screen and an overhead projector (OHP) unit. However, it may be that a laptop and portable projection unit is to be provided, in which case these items may not be permanent fixtures in the room. Some organisations may not use projection screens and instead project to a white wall.

> *MELISSA: "Why is it so dark in here?"*
> *MULDER: "The lights aren't on."*
> ***The X Files***

You may be bringing along your own laptop, in which case you should check that there is a suitable extension lead for mains power. Position the lead carefully so that, if you were to walk around a short distance during a presentation, you would not trip over it.

Depending on the purpose of your presentation, you may already know approximate audience numbers (for example, for a final year project, your audience members may consist only of academic and industrial supervisors). If you know audience numbers, and if you have the time and access to the room, you may wish to arrange furniture in a way that suits you best.

Researching...the environment

Whilst you are researching the room, pay careful attention to lighting and the room temperature. See where the light switches are and, as daft as it may sound, learn to use them if necessary. We say this as some rooms may not be fitted with the traditional "on-off" switch but may instead be equipped with "rocker"-type switches that incorporate both the on-off function and an integrated dimmer device. If so, learn how to use them properly.

Depending on the size of the room, there may be more than one switch on the panel, each controlling different lights (or rows of lights). Experiment until you are comfortable with the level of lighting (for example, some people like to turn off the middle row(s) of lights completely as this causes less glare on the projection screen). Check the location of windows. Daylight may fall awkwardly on your projection screen (causing a reflection), which you may choose to rectify.

When checking windows, see if and how they open (in some organisations, they may be sealed depending on which floor you are on, for health and safety reasons). If the room is overheated or otherwise stuffy, try to open the windows for a short while before your presentation (although this may not always be possible). You may be asked by an audience member if they can open a window for some air; once you know how to open the window, you can oblige very easily.

Researching...the equipment

> *"Make sure you know the spec. of the machine you will be working on. Some of my students developed a five-minute presentation on a high spec. machine, only to find a really old machine was being used for the actual presentation. All their highly interactive graphics with full sound took forever and they ran way over time!"*
>
> ***Dr Chris Bloor, University of Sunderland***

Have a look at the computer, the projection unit and overhead projector (should these items be in the room). Check to see whether there is an installed floppy disk unit (although these are rapidly being phased out), a CD-ROM unit, a USB connection (many presenters are now using USB memory sticks for file transportation). If you prefer, try to copy your presentation to the computer's hard disk (as the presentation often runs much quicker) before you start the presentation.

If you choose to use electronic projection, remember that it is good practice to bring OHP acetates as a backup.

Disasters do occasionally strike and it is best to be prepared. If the worst should happen (e.g. you have a major problem with your planned electronic presentation), you can revert instantly to your backup presentation.

Should something like this happen, keep your nerve, remember to smile and turn the situation around so that you are again in control. Similar things have happened to even the most experienced presenters (the authors included). Our own personal such horror story was rectified by smoothly bringing out our black-and-white backup acetates and telling the audience, "You can tell I used to be a Project Manager can't you?". Your audience will give you credit for being so well prepared as long as you do not dwell on the set-back.

Don't forget to look at and test the OHP unit. Many people have become so accustomed to electronic projection (e.g. PowerPoint®) that they have almost forgotten how to use traditional (although some would say old!) methods of projection. Remember to place your acetates (or transparencies) directly onto the platen, face-up (facing you), so that YOU can read it clearly (i.e. it should not be upside down or back-to-front). If you can read it, so can your audience.

Some presenters prefer to bring their own laptop to the presentation, often forgetting that this still needs to be connected to the projection equipment. This is not always an easy task, simple though it may seem. Physically connecting a cable between your laptop and a projector is very simple. However, it may well be that either the laptop or the projection equipment (or perhaps both) require a "cold start" before they "recognise" each other. Sometimes, it may be as simple as pressing <FUNCTION> <F5> (or similar) on your laptop, but be prepared for the fact that such simple things often taken an incredibly long time.

Researching...nerves

If you are an inexperienced presenter, then it may well be that you are nervous about the presentation. This may especially be the case if your presentation is part of an assignment or project. The key to reducing nerves is to be prepared and relaxed, two aspects that are linked.

> *"Studies show that fear of public speaking ranks higher than the fear of dying. I guess this means that most people at a funeral would rather be in the coffin than delivering the eulogy..."*
>
> ***Jerry Seinfeld, comedian***

Prepare by giving the presentation the attention and focus that it deserves; in this way, you should also feel more relaxed as you know that you have put effort into the presentation.

Index cards

Your preparation may also include producing index cards, on which you can write key points (acting as your prompts), which you may or may not decide to use during the actual presentation. If you feel yourself getting nervous and feel that you may forget what you have to say, refer to your pre-prepared cards.

Water

Some presenters like to take a bottle of water into their presentation with them. In organised conferences and workshops, jugs of ice-water, mints and so forth are often placed on tables around the room and at or near the lectern.

> *"Bring a small bottle of water with you and take regular sips in the time leading up to your presentation. This helps prevent against 'dry mouth' syndrome, the effects of pre-presentation nerves."*
>
> ***Tim Thompson, former student***

If, because of nerves, you feel your mouth and lips getting dry, take a few quick sips of water before you start the presentation. Once the presentation is underway, people generally find that any nerves evaporate.

If you have to, take a few sips of water between slides or during the question-and-answer session. We emphasise that you should take small sips rather than gulps as this may lead to you needing a toilet break.

Alcohol

Although a few sips of water is generally okay, do not be tempted to take anything stronger into your presentation. We have never actually witnessed this ourselves, but once smelt alcohol on one presenter's breath as we talked to him (after the presentation) outside the room. On questioning, he confessed that he had drunk "a couple of shots" to calm his nerves. We would advise that you do not drink alcohol shortly before the presentation (and, of course, never during it).

Sleep

Although you may be nervous, try to get enough sleep the night before your presentation. You will find that if you have prepared well for your presentation your nerves are vastly reduced – allowing you to sleep better.

the best way to combat nerves is to practice, practice, practice!

Researching...voice

It is often said that nobody likes the sound of their own voice. You may like someone else's voice (and if they hate theirs, they may like yours!).

When delivering a presentation, always use your own, natural, everyday voice. Do not be tempted to adopt a persona or voice which is patently not you. If you are delivering your presentation to supervisors (or people that you already know), your "new voice" will come as a surprise to them.

> *"By apologising during a presentation for a misspelt word or a simple mistake you are only drawing attention to it. Chances are if you don't apologise, people probably won't notice."*
>
> ***Tim Thompson, former student***

Speak clearly so that the audience can both hear and understand you. If you are unsure of this, at the beginning of your presentation, do not be afraid to ask the audience whether they can hear you clearly.

Your voice will sound much more natural if you do not read directly from a script. Reading tends to make you speak in a monotone, which is the last thing you want.

Emphasise words when you need to by slightly increasing the volume of your voice or by pausing briefly. Bear in mind that if you pause for too long, the audience may get uncomfortable or may take the opportunity to ask you a question, which may throw you off track.

If you are new to presentations, by far the best thing you can do is to practice in front of friends or family. We acknowledge that this is not easy. You may feel embarrassed, shy, may get nervous or get the giggles. If so, consider practising in front of a mirror. We know that many people don't like this either as they think it makes them look silly. We would argue that it is surely better to look silly in front of a mirror than in front of your audience.

By practising, you will be able to iron out many wrinkles in your techniques, giving you more confidence for your final presentation.

Researching...dress

We will talk about "dress" in more detail later in the book. In essence though, your dress should be as important to you as it is to your audience. The way you choose to dress should be an accurate reflection of your audience's choice of dress for a typical working day (for instance, if you are presenting a final year project in front of your industrial supervisor(s), and you know that the company's culture – and hence dress code – is informal, then you should dress as you normally do for business meetings at that organisation).

> ***"I'm sorry if my friends make a bad impression, but it's an accurate one".***
>
> ***"Drew", The Drew Carey Show***

Given that many undergraduate and postgraduate students may be preparing for life in the industrial and commercial world, the rule of thumb has always been that one should dress in a business suit/outfit for a presentation. If such a career is your objective, then by all means wear your business suit.

If your presentation is to be delivered to your academic and/or industrial supervisors, and you know that their dress preference is casual (i.e. no business suit), you may decide to dress in the same manner.

The same is also true if you definitely do not like dressing formally (even though there are shades of formality from a business suit at one end of the spectrum through to a formal dinner jacket/evening wear). There should be no compulsion for you to wear what you may consider to be a "costume" if you do not feel comfortable wearing it.

Researching...attitude

Remember that your attitude should be one of professionalism and confidence. If you know that your presentation should be business-like, then think business-like and act business-like. If your attitude does not match the thrust of your presentation, your delivery may well suffer.

> ***"Confidence is contagious. So is lack of confidence."***
>
> ***Vince Lombardi, American football coach***

Remember: turn your mobile phone off if you have one. Calls and text messages have a habit of arriving at the most inopportune moments. Remember also that off means OFF – merely putting your phone on to vibrate mode is pretty much pointless; as you may be aware, the phone will still be audible (and therefore annoying) should it ring.

Amazingly, we have attended one presentation where not only did the presenter's mobile phone ring, but then we sat open-mouthed as she said, "Excuse me" and proceeded to talk to her caller for a short time.

Researching...stage positioning

By stage positioning, we mean:

- where you choose to stand in your presentation;
- how you choose to stand.

You will need to be close to your computer or the OHP unit when you advance or change slides. Some presenters like to take a few short steps away from the computer as they feel that this brings them closer to the audience. If you choose to do this, ensure that you have a clear path and that there are no obstacles, such as extension leads, in your way.

How you choose to stand is a reflection of your attitude. We have seen many presenters who stood stiff as a board, hardly moving at all during the entire presentation. We have seen others who were more dynamic and used their hands and arms expressively throughout the presentation.

Some presenters adopt a leaning pose (almost as if they are leaning against a bar in a pub) where they lean against a wall or even the OHP or projector table (embarrassing themselves when they discover that it is on wheels...). When asked after the presentation why they had adopted this slouching position, the presenters often did not know that they had been. Some admitted that, because they were in a business suit, they thought they should act "differently".

Researching...notes/scripts

Although the use of index cards can be a good idea (as they can help you get back on track should you lose your position in the presentation), we would advise against using them as a presentation script which you read verbatim.

By using a script, you automatically become less spontaneous than you otherwise would. As mentioned earlier, a good presentation should not be delivered in a monotone but should incorporate your natural voice, with effective use of tone, inflection, emphasis and pauses.

> ***"The audience only pays attention as long as you know where you are going."***
>
> ***Philip Crosby, Management Guru***

Worse still is the presenter who, using a pre-prepared script, proceeds to hold the script in front of their face as they read it aloud. This is bad enough but the problem is compounded because, as these presenters are often the most nervous, their hands tremble with nerves, making their papers shake. Although the tremble in the fingers may be slight, it is magnified greatly by the time it reaches the end of the papers.

Researching...jokes

We are often asked whether jokes are a good idea during presentations. Whilst the use of gentle humour can be used quite effectively during most presentations, the inclusion of jokes boils down to your own personality, your audience, the context of your presentation and, of course, the type of joke.

Remember, there is a danger that:

- your joke is not funny;
- you do not tell the joke in the right way;
- your joke may be offensive; or
- you forget the punchline.

The only time that we (the authors) use jokes during our own presentations is by way of the use of humourous anecdotes. Like most anecdotes, they are illustrative in nature and are told to explain or prove a concept.

Remember that your presentation should be professional – it is not a stand-up comedy routine. If in doubt, don't use jokes at all.

Researching...pointing

For the occasional presenter, there is no need to invest in any form of pointing device. Such devices almost always used to take the form of an extendable "pen" that was pointed at the projection screen.

> *"Beware of the use of technology! When I first started using PowerPoint® I had a habit of pointing at the presenter's screen, till I realised the students couldn't see what I was pointing at."*
>
> ***Dr Chris Bloor, University of Sunderland***

Laser pointers have gained in popularity in recent years. For inexperienced presenters, we would strongly advise against the use of such devices. You will not be experienced in their use and, because of this, you run the risk of accidentally pointing the laser towards the audience. This is highly dangerous and you will not be regarded favourably by the audience.

Additionally, if you are nervous and if your hands shake, then so will the laser pointer. If it shakes all over the screen, what is the point of using it?

Try not to point at the presentation screen itself as, by doing so, your body may get in the way of somebody in the audience. If you do choose to point:

- when using electronic projection (e.g. PowerPoint®), use the mouse or built-in pointing device (on a laptop);
- when using an overhead projector, point onto the acetate sheet (lying on the projector's platen).

Researching...body language

Body language is essentially non-verbal communication and refers to both body and facial expressions, movement, gestures and attitudes. Although body language is a very complex academic area of interest, there are useful elements which can be applied to the field of presentations.

> *"It's lack of faith that makes people afraid of meeting challenges, and I believe in myself."*
>
> ***Muhammad Ali***

The way that presenters express themselves socially (and by using their arms, hands and fingers) should be complementary to the spoken delivery of the presentation content.

It may be useful to be aware of some of the most common gestures (and how these can be interpreted by your audience) without getting obsessed with them.

The following table shows some of the more common manifestations of body language and the meaning behind them:

Non-verbal behaviour	Interpretation
Brisk, erect walk	Confidence
Standing with hands on hips	Readiness, aggression
Sitting with legs crossed, foot kicking slightly	Boredom
Sitting, legs apart	Open, relaxed
Arms crossed on chest	Defensiveness
Walking with hands in pockets, shoulders hunched	Dejection
Hand to cheek	Evaluation, thinking
Touching, slightly rubbing nose	Rejection, doubt, lying
Rubbing the eye	Doubt, disbelief
Hands clasped behind back	Anger, frustration, apprehension
Locked ankles	Apprehension
Head resting in hand, eyes downcast	Boredom
Rubbing hands	Anticipation
Sitting with hands clasped behind head, legs crossed	Confidence, superiority
Open palm	Sincerity, openness, innocence
Pinching bridge of nose, eyes closed	Negative evaluation
Tapping or drumming fingers	Impatience
Steepling fingers	Authoritative
Patting/fondling hair	Lack of self-confidence; insecurity
Tilted head	Interest
Stroking chin	Trying to make a decision
Looking down, face turned away	Disbelief
Biting nails	Insecurity, nervousness
Pulling or tugging at ear	Indecision

Body language: non-verbal behaviour and interpretation

Webpage: www.deltabravo.net/custody/body.htm

Researching...accents

We are often asked by students whether their own accents will be a hindrance during their presentations. Although our overseas students ask this question the most, we are surprisingly often asked by many of our UK-based students as well (as there are of course regional accents within the UK). Students ask whether they should work on eliminating or softening their accents.

Our advice is that you should not spend time working on losing your accent, but should instead concentrate on designing and delivering the best presentation possible. In the same way that people do not like the sound of their own voice, people often do not like their accents either.

Your audience will be more concerned if you do not speak clearly or if the volume of your voice is too high or low.

Checklist

In this chapter, we have:

- explained the importance of effective research;
- assessed the elements of good presentation technique;
- examined details such as room layout, lighting and pointing.

Chapter 2

PRESENTATION CONTENT

Chapter summary

This chapter will explain how you can best decide on your presentation content. We discuss how the concept of "brainstorming" can be used to assimilate important concepts in your presentation. Some of the more helpful features of computer-based presentation packages, such as Microsoft® PowerPoint®, are presented together with a caveat.

Learning outcomes

After studying this chapter, you should be able to do the following:

Outcome 1: effectively use brainstorming techniques in order to create key concepts for use in your slides;

Outcome 2: create an effective close to your presentation;

Outcome 3: learn how to use chapter headings as a basis for slide headings;

Outcome 4: assess the inclusion of an exposition section in your presentation.

Having carried out background research into your presentation (room, attitude, dress and so forth), don't forget that you need to carry out research into your presentation content as well.

This should include research on which items to present, how best to present raw data, whether to include graphs and charts, deciding on how best to present your work (i.e. in chronological order or as a "story") and the importance of a good "open" and "close" (terms which will be explained in this chapter).

Content can be described as "functional design" and deals with the actual and implied message of your presentation. Presentation design is a complementary element (dealing with the effective delivery of these messages) and is the subject of the next chapter.

Deciding on content

Deciding on the content of your presentation may be very easy (e.g. for a final year project, your presentation content would be dictated by the content of your written report), but otherwise may be difficult or confusing for the novice presenter.

If you are confused as to where to begin, the following diagram may help you. Although it is simple, it can help to clarify matters in your own mind.

> ***"The vital ingredient of all successful presentations is meticulous planning. The presentation cycle begins at the preparation stage, where it is imperative that the content is researched fully and transcribed in detail. Facts, visuals and style should then be planned to a pre-established structure. These are the elements that could mean the difference between a tuned out audience, which will in turn affect your style and flow, and an audience educated and entertained by your presentation."***
>
> ***Alex Saunders, former student***

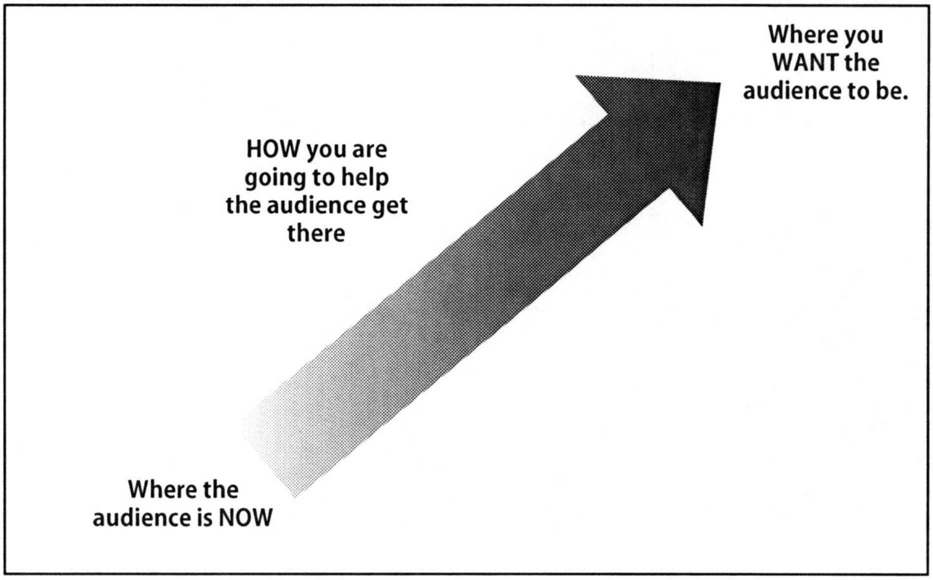

Deciding on content

It asks three very simple questions:

Question	Timeframe
Where is the level of your audience's understanding NOW?	BEFORE the presentation
Where do you want this understanding to be at the END of the presentation?	END of the presentation
HOW are you going to help the audience get there?	DURING the presentation

If you go through each of these questions in turn, you may find that you are actually faced with more questions than initial answers. This should not worry you unduly, as breaking these questions down into sub-questions can help to clarify your thinking.

A simple brainstorming technique can help to focus your ideas, triggering new thoughts but overall retaining your train of thought. It may be worth knowing that the term "brainstorming" has come under scrutiny recently as it can be considered to be a politically incorrect term. The following terminology is often used to describe exactly the same (or an inherently similar) concept.

Brainstorming	
	"mind shower"
	"mind map"
	"word storm"
	"brain dump"
	"word dump"
	"thought dump"
	"round robin"

The following can be viewed as a basic example of a brainstorm for a typical student project, in this case dealing with the analysis, design and production of a database for an external client.

Project brainstorm

aims; objectives; content; mission; research; presentation; beginning; middle;

end; analysis; problem context; understanding; design issues; usability;

user training; systems analysis; aesthetics; functionality; style; substance;

expandability; user guide; learning; training; project mark; conclusion;

recommendation; planning; project management; Gantt chart;

before and after; looking back; what went well; what went wrong; next time;

time management; presentation length; nerves; index cards; facts

Listing words in this manner can often help the novice presenter. There are often so many thoughts going round in your head that you do not know where to start and you may begin to panic.

If you look at these words, you may see an occasional pattern or thread between some or all of the words. The key is to document your thought process, however jumbled or confused you may initially believe it to be. Once you have the simple words down, they can act as a basis for refinement.

Refinement

Having carried out a brainstorm, you can then move on to refinement. This incorporates your decision whether to present chronologically (the order in which events occurred) or whether to opt for a "story" (placing the project in the context of a problem domain). Regarding a chronological order, it should be noted that very few projects are executed in the final order in which they are presented.

Whilst there are no hard or fast rules on how best to refine, students often find it easier to follow chapter headings (from their final report, project or dissertation) as a basis for their presentation.

> *"You should know equally well the subject of your presentation as well as your audience."*
>
> ***Paris Parissis, former student***

Remember that there are always three main aspects to an effective presentation: beginning, middle and end. This may appear to be obvious but it is amazing how many students fail to follow this simple structure in their presentations. We shall briefly return to these three aspects in the next section.

Chapter titles as a basis for slide headings

Your academic tutors (and/or institution) may have prescribed views on report, project or dissertation layout and may provide you with examples of such. Other tutors prefer to leave it to their students and may award a proportion of the final mark accordingly.

By way of example for a typical student project (again, this one deals with the creation of a database for a project client), the student may opt for the following chapter titles (in their written report, project or dissertation):

1. Introduction
2. Company profile
3. Current system
4. Analysis and design
5. Implementation of new system
6. Project exposition
7. Conclusion

These chapter titles can then be broadly used as slide headings for your presentation, remembering of course that there are some sections within the chapter headings, the most important aspects of which should also find their way into your presentation.

Returning back to our "beginning, middle and end" advice, we can depict this by way of the following (slightly expanded) table which shows how your chapter headings can help inform your slide headings. Note that the sub-headings (bulletpoints):

- are merely representative;
- are by no means an exhaustive list;
- may not appear as definitive sub-headings in the presentation and/or report.

Chapter (and possible slide) headings	Timescale
INTRODUCTION • Introduction to presentation • Introduction to project • Introduction to company (if applicable)	BEGINNING
COMPANY PROFILE • Introduction to company • History and profile • Location(s) • Link history to next section (slide)	
CURRENT SYSTEM • Current working practice • Workflow patterns • Systems analysis • Problems and "wish list" for new system	MIDDLE
ANALYSIS AND DESIGN • Systems analysis for proposed system • Design for proposed system • Checking of the above	
IMPLEMENTATION OF NEW SYSTEM • Criteria • Selection of application package • Implementation • Testing • Maintenance plan	
PROJECT EXPOSITION • Resources • Time management • Lessons learned • Set-backs • Project management • Evaluation	END
CONCLUSION • Success criteria • Recommendations • Future work	

Designing an effective close

When you are preparing the content of your presentation, constantly bear in mind that it should all be building up to a strong and effective closing statement. It may well be that your audience's impression of you is based entirely on the last few moments of your presentation.

We have attended many presentations ourselves, and have heard stories of many others, where the following words are typical of those spoken as closing statements:

" and, er, that's it really"

"that's all from me, folks"

"Phew, glad that's over!"

With all of the above, if you are very lucky, the audience may hear an unenthusiastic and watery addition of "...Erm, any questions?". We cover the subject of questions later on the book, but you should be actively prepared for questions. A good presentation can be ruined by a presenter who, as they pack up their personal belongings, ask "are there any questions"? You have just sent out a signal to your audience that you are not interested in any questions at all.

Or, worse still, there may be no closing statement at all! As an example of this, the presentation peters out with the PowerPoint® projection finishing abruptly (returning to the PowerPoint® application, not the slideshow view); it is this, and only this, which informs the audience that the presentation is now at an end.

> *"Although it's good to include humour within a presentation sometimes, its use should be assessed for its relevance and understanding. Be careful of presentations given to an audience whose first language may not be the same as the presenter's (e.g. a presentation to a German audience given in English). What's funny in one language may be confusing, misleading and incomprehensible in another..."*
>
> ***Jonathan Murphy, former student***

Remember that you have worked tremendously hard in preparing for the presentation – don't let all that hard work be for nothing. Have a strong closing statement prepared. As an example of an effective close:

**"I have now come to the end of my presentation.
I hope you enjoyed it and found it to be informative.
I would be pleased to take any questions."**

Note

We cannot emphasise enough that you should not try to remember this particular example closing statement verbatim – try to design your own statement, tailored to your presentation verbatim.

Headings

Whether you are using PowerPoint® or not, remember to give each of your slides a clear and concise heading. If you can, make sure that this heading ideally fits onto one line, and that you use the same font, colour and size for headings throughout the presentation.

Bulletpoints

We talk more about the design of bulletpoints in the next chapter, but it is worth mentioning how useful bulletpoints can be when displaying content.

If used correctly, bulletpoints can be a very clear way of presenting text-based data and information. Keep text as brief as possible (making sure that it still makes sense) and then try to talk "around" the main point. The bulletpointed text should act as a trigger which reminds you to talk (in your normal and natural voice) in more detail about that particular aspect.

Do not be tempted to merely read out the bulletpointed text – your audience will be able to do that for themselves. By way of example, the following diagram shows how to and how not to present the same content.

Introduction

- Lexden Publishing – based in Colchester
- The project – basically what I did
- Current system – what was bad
- Implemented System – what went well
- Exposition – what I learnt
- Summary – a conclusion

The wrong way

Introduction

Lexden Publishing
The project
Current system
Implemented System
Exposition
Summary

The right way

As you can see, the "wrong" example looks cluttered and contains too much information, some of which is redundant. The "right" example contains the most important information from the "wrong" example and yet is clear, concise and professional.

There is no need to display extra information that can be easily "talked around" existing words. For example, the slide will display the words "Lexden Publishing" whilst you say something like: "My project was to design and implement a new royalty database for my client Lexden Publishing who are based in Colchester".

By electing not to use physical bulletpoints (●), but keeping the "lines" created by them and by using short words (without the unnecessary explanation given on the "wrong" example), we are left with sufficient white space that could be used to insert a complementary picture.

Bells and whistles

One of the many pitfalls of new technology (such as Microsoft® PowerPoint®) is the temptation to use all of the functionality, whether it is appropriate or not. Bitmaps (pictures), sounds and animated graphics (GIFs) have often proved to be too much of a temptation for the inexperienced presenter.

Bitmap images

Microsoft® PowerPoint® comes bundled with various categories of bitmap images, that can be used freely by the presenter. There are third party sources (some of which charge for their services) which also supply suitable graphics.

As a caveat, we would warn against using graphics which look tacky, out of place or which are inappropriate to a particular slide. Additionally we would recommend that a maximum of one graphic (if appropriate) per slide is more than enough. If you use too many on one slide, the audience concentrate their attention on these, losing focus on both your words and your speech.

Sounds

Microsoft® PowerPoint® also comes bundled with several sound effects. Unless sound is vital to your presentation (for example, your project was on a sound-based or video-based problem), best practice recommends that sound is largely avoided. We have seen several presentations where bulletpointed text was "revealed" letter by letter, accompanied by a raucous machine-gun sound.

> ***"Computers make it easier to do a lot of things, but most of the things they make it easier to do don't need to be done."***
>
> ***Andy Rooney, American journalist and commentator***

Not only was the sound far too loud for the room but the presenter, on seeing our discomfort, asked whether he should turn the sound effect off. When we confirmed this he then spent an agonising two minutes looking through the various PowerPoint® options trying to turn the sound off. He therefore lost control of the presentation, and with it, also lost our empathy and interest in the rest of his presentation.

Animated GIFs

There are many Internet sites offering free, downloadable, animated graphics. The overwhelming majority are tacky beyond words and they very quickly lose their limited power to amuse. If you happen to find one which is suitable for inclusion in your presentation, be aware that your audience's attention may be unduly distracted should they concentrate on this graphic – they are therefore not paying full attention to either you or your presentation.

Animated effects

Microsoft® PowerPoint® again comes bundled with custom animation effects which, to the novice presenter, are very attractive. If you opt for animation effects (for example, text which flies in from various parts of the screen), bear in mind that this can be distracting for your audience. Additionally, if used too often, it can be boring (as the audience now knows what to expect).

So, in summary, just because technology comes with various options, does not mean that you necessarily have to use them all (or, in fact, any).

With all of the above, simpler is often best.

Project exposition

When writing your final report, some academic tutors like to see a chapter or section on how your project went as a process (an exposition). If you have included such a chapter, remember to include an exposition section in your presentation as well.

Typically, an exposition would comprise honest descriptions of:

- what went well in your project;
- what went badly in your project;
- what you personally learnt from the project process;
- what you should have done differently;
- what you thought of your product (a product in the context of a computing-based project may be a database).

Such a section would normally end with a reflective look back on the project process. If you were to start the project from scratch tomorrow morning, what would you plan differently knowing what you know now?

> *"Experience is simply the name we give our mistakes."*
> ***Oscar Wilde***

It should be emphasised that a project exposition chapter or section is good practice that was instilled into us as students (and practice which we pass on to our own students), but preferences do vary from institution to institution. It is always worth checking with your academic tutor before including such a chapter in your final report or such a section in your presentation.

Opening and conclusion slide

It is good practice to open your presentation with an "agenda" slide which can be as simple as a headings list of the slides you are about to run through (whether these are PowerPoint® or OHP-based). Such an opening slide sets the scene for your presentation and sends out a signal to your audience that you are prepared and have researched.

If you are apprehensive about your presentation, seeing this agenda slide reminds you that you have worked hard at this point, you have researched well and you are fully prepared to deliver this presentation – you therefore should have no reason to feel nervous.

> *"Before starting the actual presentation, give the audience an indication of what they are going to hear and make sure that you have a conclusion or review of what you said."*
>
> ***Ameneh Mojtabai, former student***

Likewise, your final slide should act as a conclusion or summary of your presentation. It should contain the most important points of your presentation, particularly the ones that you want the audience to take away with them.

Script –v– cards

Once you have a firm idea of your presentation content, you can begin to concentrate on how best to remember it. We would always advise against using a formal script but, if you are inexperienced or nervous, would recommend that you prepare cue cards which can prompt you should you forget what to say. As your experience and confidence grows, you can discard the cue cards completely and use your bulletpoints as an effective prompt.

> *"Eighty per cent of success is showing up."*
>
> ***Woody Allen, comedian and film maker***

Checklist

In this chapter, we have:

- examined the efficacy of the "brainstorming" approach;
- analysed how best to refine outcomes from such an exercise;
- appreciated the prospect of including an exposition section in your presentation.

Chapter 3

PRESENTATION DESIGN

Chapter summary

This chapter explains the importance of a good and effective presentation design. Various types of presentation media are presented and discussed. Good practice on use of fonts is provided and debated.

Learning outcomes

After studying this chapter, you should be able to do the following:

Outcome 1: understand the importance of effective presentation design;

Outcome 2: present both your concept and yourself in an effective manner;

Outcome 3: make an informed choice as to the most appropriate presentation media for your presentation;

Outcome 4: decide on the most effective font, colour and font size.

When one thinks of presentations, the first thing that generally comes to mind is an image of a presenter in front of a screen on which is projected an electronic presentation courtesy of Microsoft® PowerPoint®.

While there is no doubt that such innovations have radically altered the way in which both academics and industrialists design and deliver presentations, many presenters have fallen into the trap of relying too much on technology.

> *"It usually takes more than three weeks to prepare a good impromptu speech."*
>
> ***Mark Twain***
> ***(1835 – 1910)***

The most common result of this is a presentation which, although initially pleasing to the eye, is lacking in actual content or, worse still, a presentation which is remembered more for colours, animation and sounds than the content (which is what the audience actually came for). This is often referred to as "PowerPoint® overkill".

The key is to use such technology to complement your presentation, remembering of course that it is you who should be in charge of your presentation and not the technology.

The previous chapter has looked at functional design; this chapter will look at the other complementary design aspect: aesthetical design. Aesthetical design is essentially "style" and deals with colour schemes, fonts and so forth.

Design for whom? You, the audience or both?

It is very easy to lose sight of the presentation's objectives, particularly if you rely too heavily on computer-based presentation tools. Who should the presentation be designed for? You? Your audience? Additionally, do you "project" your own image? Or do you tailor the presentation toward your audience's preferences? Or both?

Your target audience will alter the direction and focus of your presentation design. It is vitally important that you know as soon as possible who the target audience will be so that you can tailor and focus your presentation accordingly.

Audience design

For an academic presentation, the target audience would almost certainly be your academic supervisors and, in the case of a company-based project, may also include your industrial supervisor or company sponsor. Design for an academic audience therefore requires some research on the presenter's part.

For most academic presentations, it is almost certain that you would have had interaction and discussion with at least one of your project supervisors beforehand (for example, during your project period).

For projects which were company-based, it is likely that you would have had interaction with at least one staff member, who may also be invited to your presentation.

You therefore have some idea as to the composition of your audience and can pitch your presentation accordingly. If there are to be additional persons present, then you should not be tempted to radically alter your presentation to please one audience member's perceived preferences – particularly when you do not know anything about this person, their position, their preferences or, in fact, whether they will actually attend.

> *"I once attended a presentation where the speaker's opening slide featured a background with an animated waterfall, the effect of which was visually stunning – unfortunately, I don't remember what the presentation was about."*
>
> ***Professor Brian Lehaney, Coventry University***

During your discussions with your academic supervisors, it should be possible to glean some insight into academic preferences, audience composition and so on. If no information is forthcoming, or perhaps is unknown, the best advice is to err on the side of caution.

If your project is dealing with "traditional" academic concepts (such as a marketing plan, business proposal etc.), then traditional background, fonts and colours should be used.

We have attended presentations which are based in "new" organisations (for example, "e-commerce"-type firms, where innovation and freshness was emphasised and the presentation style was in line with the company image. Colours, fonts and backgrounds were slightly different in as much they were more vibrant (than traditional colours), reflecting the company image and meeting with their approval.

Design to project your image

Projecting your image means injecting a little of your own persona into the presentation. After all, if the audience is not enthused by your own enthusiasm, there is no real reason for them to be impressed by your presentation or its content.

> *"There are always three speeches for every one you actually gave. The one you practiced, the one you gave, and the one you wish you gave."*
>
> ***Dale Carnegie, Management Guru***

Your image may also be that of a company if, for example, you are presenting the results of a final year, company-based, project. In this case, it may be best to use the company's colour schemes, fonts etc. Your company may have a ready-made PowerPoint® template that you can use, complete with company logo on all slides.

If you have free reign as to which fonts, colours and style you can use, try to use those colours and fonts with which you are relatively comfortable and which you think the audience will also like. There is a stereotypical view that academics are conventional and traditional. Whilst this is not always the case, the fonts and colours that you use should be both aesthetically pleasing and professional. There is therefore no need to use the entire colour palette or use every font available to you.

Projecting your image is not just limited to design of your slides and handouts. Design of your image also includes the way that you choose to dress and act.

> *"What a strange power there is in clothing."*
>
> ***Isaac Bashevis Singer, Nobel Laureate, 1978***

We have mentioned before that you should inject a little of your own persona into the presentation and that you should speak as you normally would (i.e. not be tempted to act or speak in a manner which patently is not you). Additionally, the style of dress that you choose should also be one with which you are comfortable (*see later*).

Design for the audience and yourself

Having discussed how best to design for the audience and yourself, it would seem apparent that what you need to aim for is the middle ground. Find a suitable design which will:

a) not alienate your chosen audience; and

b) also be the one that you are most comfortable with.

Dress

Traditional convention dictates that presentations are quite formal in nature and therefore quite serious. This seriousness requires a professional attitude and presenters would normally dress in an appropriately formal manner, i.e. a business suit.

Whilst there is no hard and fast rule as to the way you should dress, we would advise that you dress as you would for an interview.

Generally, this would include wearing a business suit (with shirt and tie for the men, formal top for the ladies). Much as you would prepare for an interview, make sure that you are as presentable as possible ensuring that shoes, hair, teeth and clothes are clean.

When we tell our students (in the classroom) or our delegates (on short courses) about such level of detail, we are sometimes greeted with a raised eyebrow or two from a minority. However, we have received favourable comments and emails after people have carried out our advice. From this feedback, it is clear that people feel better about themselves once they are freshly showered, shaved and dressed in a professional manner. This attitude carries over into your presentation.

We emphasise that this is a rule of thumb and, when in doubt, you should err on the side of caution. Again, if at all possible, try to find out beforehand what your supervisor – and indeed the audience generally – prefers. If it is not possible to ask, some initiative goes a long way. For instance, you may know the audience members by sight in which case you will be able to see their preferred style of dress, which may influence your own final choice.

Talking to a few academic colleagues it is clear that, whilst marks are not necessarily given for the effort of wearing a business suit, there is a strong likelihood of deducting marks for slovenly appearance. We say again that if you feel good (something that decent clothes may help you achieve), the more confident your delivery should be during your presentation. Remember that clothes maketh the (wo)man...

Godfrey:	*As for your appearance, what will you wear?*
Jim:	*What do you suggest?*
Godfrey:	*A dark suit represents traditional values.*
Jim:	*Fine, dark suit.*
Godfrey:	*But a light suit looks business-like.*
Jim:	*What about a lightish jacket with a darkish waistcoat?*
Godfrey:	*I think that would look as though you've got an identity problem.*

"The Ministerial Broadcast", Yes, Prime Minister, BBC TV

Visual aids

Visual aids come in many forms and, if used correctly, enhance the audience's understanding and enjoyment of your presentation. If used correctly they should give you confidence, allowing you to project yourself better to the audience. In this manner, the audience is more likely to remember both you and the presentation.

There are many different types of visual aids, each with advantages and disadvantages, which will now be discussed.

OHPs

Overhead projector slides (OHPs) are sometimes referred to as overhead transparencies (OHTs), acetates or foils. These come in two basic types, one which can be written on using a felt-based pen and the second, which can be printed on via a laser printer.

The chief advantages of OHPs are that they are useful and accessible for all sizes of audience (small, medium and large). Additionally, they are easy to create and use and are cost-effective.

Among the disadvantages is the fact that they often force some presenters to adhere to too rigid a presentation format. For the inexperienced presenter, this often means that they lose control of the presentation.

Electronic projection (Microsoft® PowerPoint®, etc.)

Practically the gold standard in both academic and industrial settings, this is where computer technology (such as Microsoft® PowerPoint®) is used to design and deliver the presentation.

The chief advantage of using electronic projection is virtual standardisation and, if designed correctly, a highly professional delivery. As the cost of projection equipment continues to fall, this format is being used for both formal and informal presentations.

> *"The main advice I always give on presentation skills is not to read out your presentation, but to use PowerPoint® as your prompt. That way it looks much more natural."*
>
> ***Dr Chris Bloor, University of Sunderland***

The main disadvantage of using PowerPoint® (or similar) is the temptation to go overboard – using many unnecessary tricks and functions, which runs the risk of losing focus on the salient points of the presentation.

Flip charts

Although not always available, flip charts can be used as an effective presentation medium. They are very useful as a secondary presentation medium, allowing the presenter to break off from the main presentation, perhaps to explain a concept in greater detail. This allows the presenter to focus on important points, whilst allowing the audience to look somewhere else (not just at the "primary" presentation area).

For maximum effect, flip charts should be written before the presentation. The audience may grow restless if you are to write many lines of text. In addition to this, if you were to write in front of the audience, your back would be facing them, which is regarded as bad presentation practice.

Blackboards or whiteboards, if available, can substitute for a flip chart.

Posters

Used mainly for academic conferences and symposia, posters can be used as a highly effective presentation medium. They are relatively cheap, can be designed and printed in different sizes and are therefore both efficient and effective.

Whilst they are highly interactive (the presenter stands in front of the poster and explains the chief concepts to the audience), they can be difficult to carry around (because of their length). However, if you do it right, they can look great. Microsoft® PowerPoint® (or similar) can be used to create posters using the custom size option.

Which one should you use?

Although not always possible (because of the equipment present in the room), it is always a good idea to use a combination of at least two of the presentation media already described. As mentioned earlier, this means that one medium (perhaps PowerPoint®) can be used for the main presentation whilst another can be used to concentrate on specific points and provide a welcome change of pace.

> *"A wrong decision is better than indecision."*
> ***Tony Soprano***
> ***The Sopranos***

Using two media can often help to break the monotony, giving you the opportunity to walk a short distance (allowing you to stretch your legs – possibly preventing cramp). Remember that the audience will "walk with you", thus heightening their concentration. Some people like to use the flip chart (or black/whiteboard) to answer questions from the audience.

Design of visual aids

An audience is more likely to be interested in what you say, and perhaps be persuaded by your arguments, if you use visual aids. By allowing them to hear and see what you are saying, they are more likely to remember the main points of your presentation. By showing that you have gone to the trouble of preparing slides etc., the audience's perception of you is enhanced.

Remember that an average presenter using visual aids can sometimes be better than a good one who does not use any.

Colour schemes

If at all possible, try to use colour in your presentation. There is a cut-off point of course and one of the problems with using technology such as PowerPoint® is the temptation to use the full palette of colours available. There is no need to do this as you will find that using a consistent colour scheme throughout is much more pleasant for your audience.

Perhaps the best advice at this point is to **KISS**. This simple acronym stands for:

Keep
It
Simple
Stupid

By remembering this word, hopefully your presentations will not only possess a consistent colour scheme, but will also be remembered by your audience.

If you choose to use graphs, bar charts, pie charts etc., remember to keep these as simple as you possibly can. Since you are using colour, your graphs should also be in colour if at all possible.

> *"Just because I don't know doesn't mean I don't understand."*
>
> ***Homer Simpson, The Simpsons***

It goes without saying that colour content should be kept tasteful and professional at all times. However, this is easier said than done. What one person considers tasteful, another may regard as awful. By all means look at other peoples' presentation styles for pointers but do try to develop your own. This way you can be sure that you are delivering your own presentation and not just acting the part of somebody else.

Bulletpoints are much preferred to paragraphs of text. When we talk of bulletpoints, these can be visible or invisible, i.e. the lines of text are not preceded by a bullet but the distinction between lines is still clear (*see below*).

Remember

- Use colour if you can
- Make sure that colours are tasteful
- KISS!
- Graphs can be useful
- An average presenter who uses visual aids can be better than one who uses none

Slide with bulletpoints

Remember

Use colour if you can

Make sure that colours are tasteful

KISS!

Graphs can be useful

An average presenter who uses visual aids can be better than one who uses none

Slide without bulletpoints

Which font do you use?

Students sometimes have difficulties in choosing an appropriate font (and font size) for their presentations. As we have said previously, because of the growing use of computers, there is a temptation by some students to use all or nearly all of the plethora of fonts available to them. This is not a good idea. It is always best to aim for consistency, style and good taste.

There are no hard and fast rules as to which font you should choose or, indeed, which is best for an academic audience. Our own preference, as seen in the example slides above, is to opt for an Arial-type font for the main text and something like Arial Black for the slide heading. We have found that this simple approach has served us well through the years in both academic and industrial environments. We feel that the fonts are clean and visible.

We acknowledge that some academics disagree. Some favour a font such as Times New Roman, the argument often being that this is the font most used in the academic environment (it is often used for journal papers and conference proceedings) as well as for internal and external communication. Additionally these same tutors feel that, as academics, it is their job to pass good practice on to their students (i.e. the use of Times New Roman).

Our reasoning for using Arial (and Arial Black) instead of Times New Roman boils down to simple clarity. Essentially, there are two "families" of font: serif and sans serif ("sans" means without).

Sans serif	Serif
Arial	Times New Roman
Arial Black	Georgia
Verdana	Book Antiqua

Examples of different types of font

Serifs are the small lines which are at the top and bottom of letters (e.g. A, B and C). The presence of these small lines makes text easier to read as the serifs guide the eye along the line of text. A serif font is primarily used for large bodies of text, whilst sans serif fonts are used for headings, subheadings and small blocks of text. The following diagram makes clear the distinction between these two families of font.

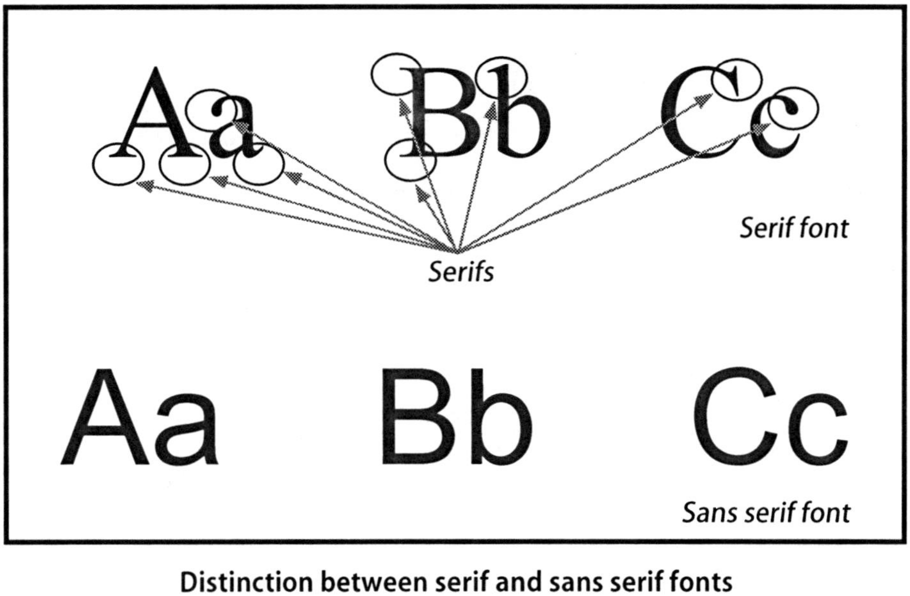

Distinction between serif and sans serif fonts

Given the size of text that one would use in a presentation, it would appear that either **serif** or **sans serif** font could be used. They both appear to be clear and crisp.

Presentation Skills

40 point, sans serif font

Presentation Skills

24 point, sans serif font

Presentation Skills

10 point, sans serif font

Presentation Skills

8 point, sans serif font

Sans serif font in different point sizes

The problem arises when a smaller font size is used. Admittedly, you should not use too small a text size (in whichever font) for presentations. Depending on the size of the room, and the audience's position in it, especially if they are sat at the rear of a medium-to-large room, a serif font would be much harder to read than a sans serif one.

Presentation Skills

40 point, sans serif font

Presentation Skills

24 point, sans serif font

Presentation Skills

10 point, sans serif font

Presentation Skills

8 point, sans serif font

Sans serif font in different point sizes

PowerPoint's pre-installed templates

A word of caution. Microsoft® PowerPoint® comes with several integrated presentation templates which many inexperienced presenters are tempted to use. Be aware that, whilst some of the colour schemes may be to your liking, the presentations are actually geared towards specific goals which are highly American in their outlook and approach (e.g. the AutoContent Wizard for Reporting Progress). We have seen several presentations where students have adopted one of these as a template for their presentation with no real understanding of the precepts, only to be caught out during questioning.

Handout slides

We are often asked by our students whether they should distribute handouts to their audience. We consider it good presentation practice to distribute handouts. Your supervisor(s) may have several presentations in a day or in a week and may welcome the chance to "revisit" your presentation when they come to mark.

Our experience, however, has also shown that some academic supervisors do not like handouts as they feel they are irrelevant and/or a waste of paper. If you possibly can, try to ask your supervisor(s) well beforehand whether your audience (or at very least your first supervisor) would welcome a handout.

If you decide to use handouts, use the PowerPoint® "handouts" function to print off replicas of your slide. Remember to select this when you print, otherwise you will print out full size copies of your slides. Try to print three to six slides per page. Any more than six on the page and they become difficult to read.

Another item of good practice is to distribute full size (i.e. full slide) handouts for slides which contain details that the audience may miss (e.g. a complex graph or diagram).

A word on the DDA

As you may be aware, the UK has introduced the *Disability Discrimination Act (DDA)*. Higher Education Institutes now have a legal duty not to discriminate against disabled people, whether they are employees (*DDA* Part 2), students, including potential and actual applicants, part-time and 'occasional' students (*DDA* Part 4) or members of the public (*DDA* Part 3).

This may or not affect how you design and deliver your presentation. There was a trend amongst some experienced educators and presenters to switch from their preferred sans serif "Arial" font to "Comic Sans" (another sans serif font). *DDA* literature often makes mention of the fact that text should ideally be in Arial or Comic Sans fonts and perhaps this explains the trend.

Not everyone likes the Comic Sans font though. Some opinions are that although it may be readable, it doesn't always look professional or "business like". As with so many things, it boils down to personal preference (*see the following figure*).

Presentation Skills

Arial font, 35 point

Presentation Skills

Arial font, 25 point

Presentation Skills

Comic Sans MS font, 35 point

Presentation Skills

Comic Sans MS font, 25 point

Sans serif fonts : comparing Arial and Comic Sans MS

Try to adopt good practice by presenting a good size, clear, readable font with equally readable handouts. You may or not know whether any audience member requires fonts to be in a certain size or would welcome full-size handouts unless they specifically ask for this (which may be during or after the presentation). If you receive this request, oblige by asking whether providing full size copies of your presentation would be acceptable.

Checklist

In this chapter, we have:

- discussed the importance of effective presentation design;
- argued the case for presenting both your concept and yourself in an effective manner;
- presented different types of (and the most commonly available) presentation media;
- debated the importance of effective fonts, colours and font sizes.

Chapter 4

KEEPING AUDIENCE INTEREST

Chapter summary

This chapter covers some of the essential ways in which you can help keep the audience interested in your presentation. We discuss how best to get the audience's attention and, once you have it, how to keep it.

Learning outcomes

After studying this chapter, you should be able to do the following:

Outcome 1: recognise and appreciate the importance of getting off to a good start in your presentation;

Outcome 2: understand the importance of a good beginning, and know how to capture your audience's attention, how to emphasise the problem, how to examine solutions and how to conclude in a succinct manner;

Outcome 3: be familiar with the basic concepts of good eye contact, facial expressions, voice and "stage" movement;

Outcome 4: review how to field audience questions and how best to effectively answer them.

In the beginning...

Remember that audience anticipation and interest is at a peak at the start of presentation. This is a chance for the audience (academic or industrial) to appraise you. They are automatically trying to judge whether you are worth listening to, whether you are any good and what they are going to learn from this presentation. Think about the presentations you have attended – what were your thoughts as the presenter was setting up?

> ***"Public speaking is very easy..."***
>
> ***Dan Quayle (to reporters, October 1988)***

The beginning of a presentation is of paramount importance. It is your best opportunity to engage with your audience and to capture their attention, and you should plan on how best to use this to your advantage. There are a few key points to remember at the beginning of your presentation which include some or all of the following:

Introduce yourself

This is essential. Make sure that you provide a good, solid introduction to yourself – include your name (you will be amazed at how many people forget to introduce themselves), academic institution (or course/module) or company (or "mock" company if you are in an academic setting).

Credence

If possible, say something that provides some evidence as to why the audience should listen to you (e.g. "My industrial placement was with the number one recruitment agency in the UK for marketing-based positions."). This is not essential though – you will know yourself, according to your particular context, whether it is appropriate or not (for example, this may not be required in a research-based final year project presentation).

Objectives

An effectively planned and concise statement of your objectives is often appropriate: some people like to present the problems first (as a reminder to the audience – and themselves) before going on to explain how they intend to deal with them. Provide a reason as to why it is in the audience's interest to listen to you (for example, "I will explain how this database can be used to save the University 25% in resources in the first year.").

> ***"Personality goes a long way."***
>
> ***Jules Pitt (Samuel L Jackson), Pulp Fiction***

Timing and control

Give an honest estimate of how long you expect to take and whether you would prefer to take questions at the end of the presentation. In a conference environment, ask the agreement of the chairman/timekeeper first – remember that YOU are in control of the presentation – act accordingly.

Main body

Where we had got to last time

Remind the audience of the current position and where you left off previously (if you had a last meeting/presentation).

Emphasise the problem

Go over the central issues and go on to discuss possible solutions. If at all possible, use numbers, facts and figures or at least quantify and qualify your answers. The audience will want you to "cut to the chase" as soon as possible. They will remember hard facts and perhaps figures – it's what they are waiting for in your presentation.

Progress and action

Show what has been achieved since the last meeting (if there was one) and state whether your project is in front of schedule, on time or behind schedule. Be honest enough to present a précis of significant problems, their impact and mitigating factors. If something can be solved, state this.

There is always a temptation to blame shortcomings on other people or things, e.g. for academic presentations: a virus on the computer, print room closed, etc. – this is a sign of poor project management on your part. You should anticipate such problems and plan accordingly. The audience is aware that such things generally happen; however, make sure that you don't pass the buck – this is a sign of weakness and indicates that you do not have full control of the project. The audience wants to know what the problems were and how you effectively overcame them.

If there were no mitigating factors, tell the audience this – it at least demonstrates that you have considered them.

Solutions

Audiences (be they academic or industrial) like solutions or answers to questions and it is your job to provide these to them. When doing so, make sure that you offer pros and cons for each solution that you present. The audience will appreciate the detail of your answer and it will confirm to them that you have thought in detail about the ramifications. Additionally, demonstration of such foresight will make the audience think (hopefully correctly) that the rest of your project is just as sound.

Recommendations

At the end of your presentation, bring together all the key points of your presentation (or argument) and present a business case (or academic argument) for your solution(s). Try to be honest – most recommendations have a "cost" or some sort of limitation. Acknowledging this demonstrates your evaluation skills and should be appreciated by your audience.

Ending the presentation

In concluding the presentation, reiterate how your company/client will benefit (or has already benefitted). For academic presentations, you should try to state what you have learnt during the project. Tell the audience how you have "grown" (allowing them to judge your personal and professional development).

Ensure that you make a good, clear, closing statement (e.g. "As you can see, if we implement this proposal, we should see cost savings of £25,000 over two years.").

Last, but by no means least, invite questions from the audience. Remember to ask if there are any questions. There is a temptation to collect together your papers and belongings while you ask – this indicates to the audience that you are not interested in their questions; they are then less likely to ask them – this is not a good thing.

> ***"Tell 'em what you're going to say.***
> ***Say it. Tell 'em what you said."***
> ***Anon***

The eyes have it

Remember to engage with your audience by looking at them. There is nothing more irritating to an audience than a presenter who:

- does not look at them at all;
- looks at one person only;
- looks at a fixed point at the rear of the room;
- presents to the screen (not looking forward at all);
- reads off a sheet of paper.

So, remember to look at your audience by looking at one person for a few seconds and then moving on to another. With practice, you will be able to project yourself in a way that everyone believes that you are delivering the presentation just for them. Do not eyeball anyone though!

Using your voice

Okay, so nobody likes the sound of their own voice – this is nothing new. However, generally the only person that does not like your voice is you – everyone else copes with it... so perhaps there is nothing wrong with it?

When delivering an effective presentation, considered use of your voice is required. You must:

- be loud enough to be heard (but not too loud);
- be clear (no mumbling);
- use pauses at the right time (but not in an overtly dramatic manner);
- learn how tone, inflection and pitch can be used to your best advantage.

All of this has to be balanced against the possibility of you sounding like an actor – it is vital that you inject "yourself" into the presentation and not another persona which patently is not you.

TIPS: Using your voice

TIP 1 **You need to be heard – you may have to adapt your voice according to the size of the room, the number of people in the audience, whether there is a microphone present or not.**

TIP 2 **Don't try to speak in a monotone voice – this is more likely to happen if you read from a pre-prepared script (this is why bullet-points are preferred – you then talk "around" the topics in your usual voice with its inherent mannerisms).**

TIP 3 **Learn how to use pauses to good effect – bear in mind that you are not delivering a dramatic monologue! Shakespearean-type pauses (the length of which is such that you risk being interrupted with a question or comment) will make your audience feel uncomfortable. Effective use of pauses allows the audience to digest your central message (and shows that you are thinking about your topic).**

Use of props

Depending on the context of your presentation (e.g. if you have been involved with the development and production of a physical end product), it may be relevant to bring a sample of the product with you (depending on its size of course). For example, a student presenting on his/her year-long project year in an engineering firm producing thermocouples, may choose to bring one or two small thermal instruments to show the audience.

NOTE

Props are not essential, but can add to the audience's interest in you and your presentation. Remember though that any prop you choose to bring to show the audience should be interesting and relevant to the context of your presentation.

Moving around

Depending on the type of presentation you are giving, it may not be appropriate to stand behind a lectern or stand. Such items act as a psychological barrier between you and the audience.

Learn to treat these items as a "line". In fact, even if you are not standing behind a lectern, there is an invisible line between the audience and the area from which you are delivering your presentation. You should be prepared to cross that line.

The most effective presentations we have attended are those where the presenter is prepared to cross this line. The presenter elects to have two or three physical positions from which to speak or explain concepts. For example, position 1 would be where the main presentation is delivered; position 2 is where the presenter may decide to use a different presentation media, e.g. a flip-chart, etc. (*see Chapter 3: Presentation Design*) and position 3 may be where the presenter chooses to answer questions.

These positions allow the audience to keep interest in your presentation as their eyes move from the normal, static position and allow you to vary pace, change your emphasis and move yourself about (this also stops you getting restless).

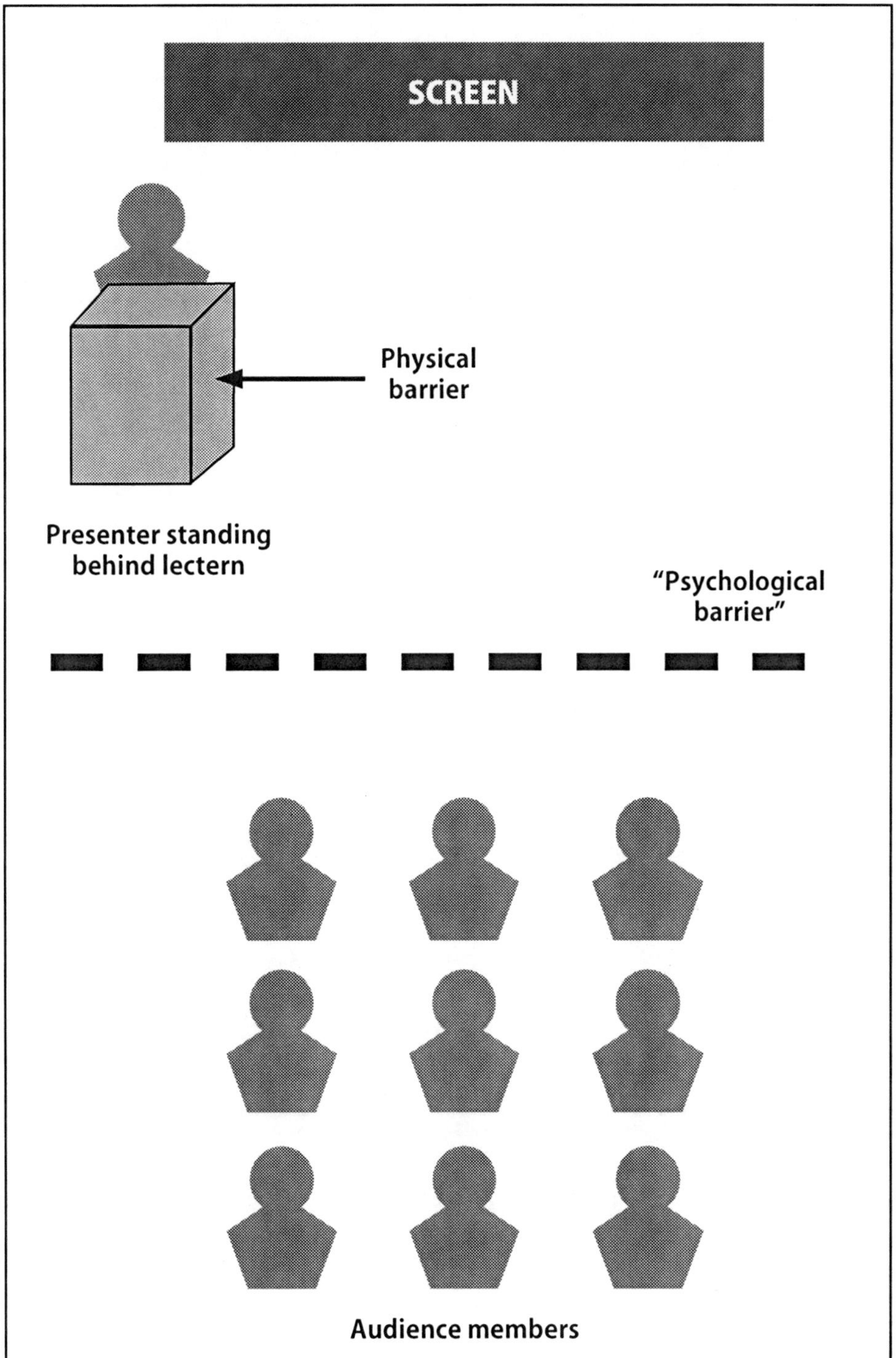

Physical barrier (standing behind a lectern)

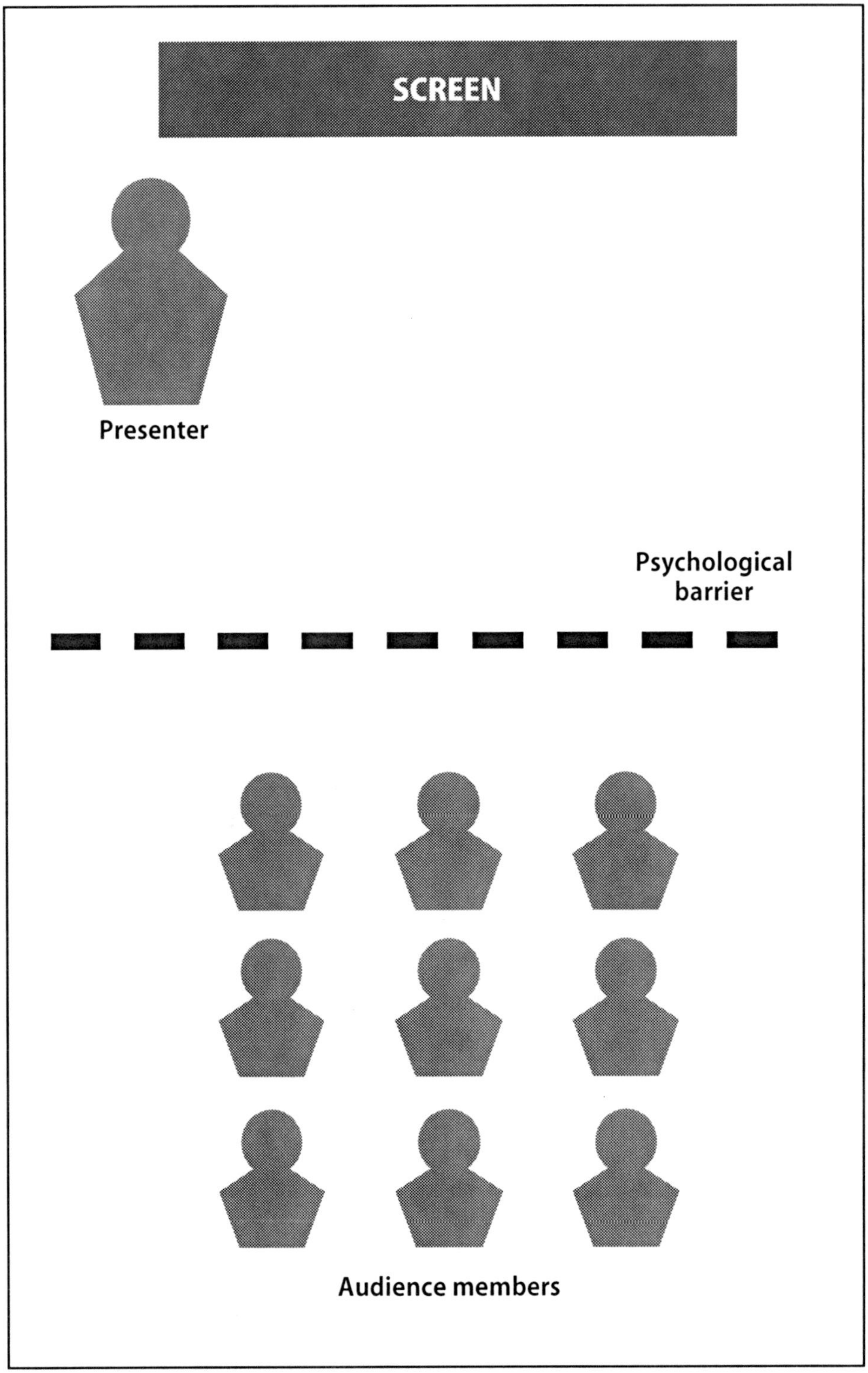

Psychological barrier without standing behind a lectern

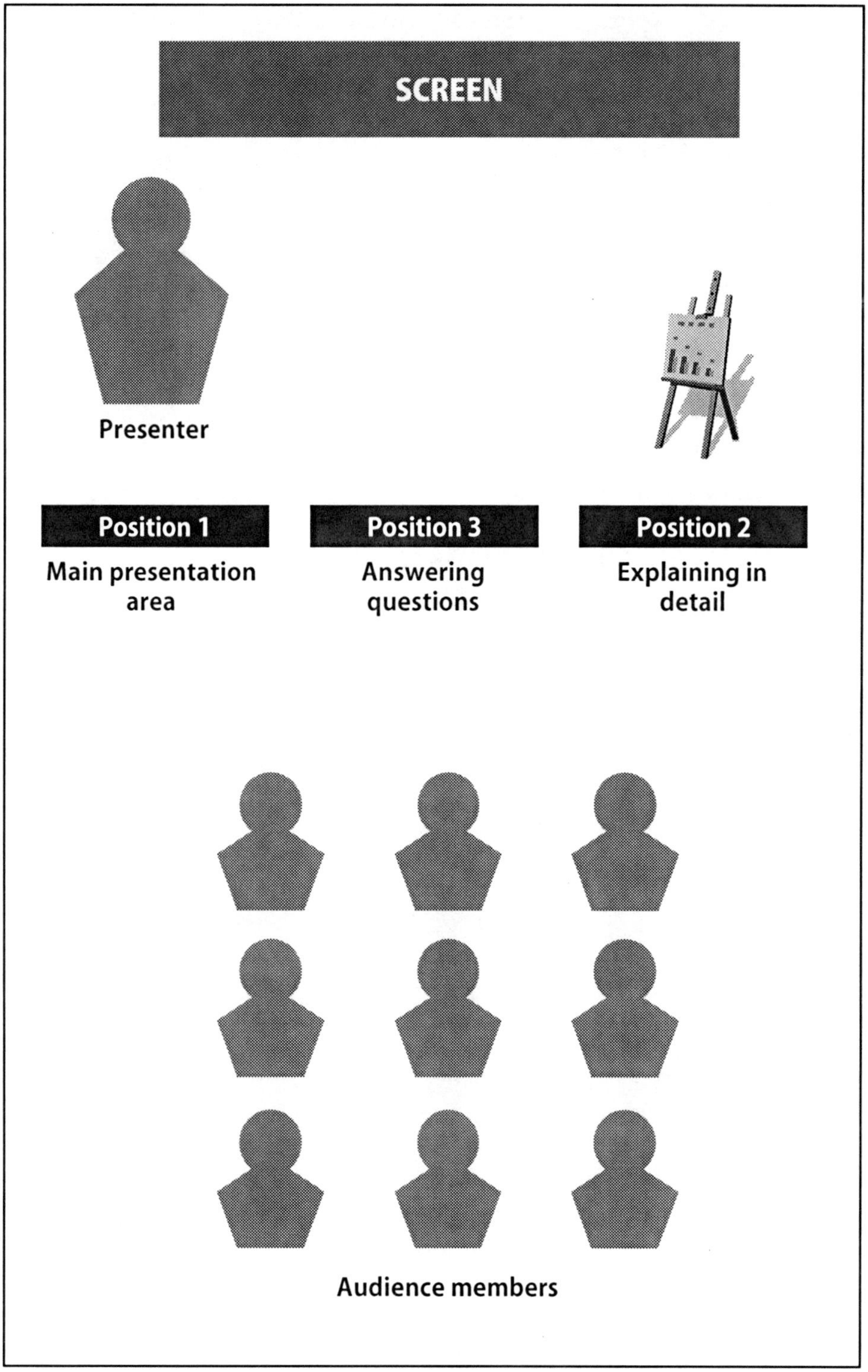

The ideal scenario (varied positions)

Questions: the ones you ask of yourself and the audience

There are many respected academics who do not like to see questions (rhetorical or otherwise) in your essays, dissertations and theses. However, in a presentation, they should be seen as a valuable tool. Such questions are ones that you ask yourself and the audience (but you don't always wait for an answer).

Questions can be used to link between different sections or aspects of your presentation. Such "in-presentation" questions should of course be directly relevant to your presentation. The key, though, is to remember that such questions should be followed by an answer. Examples of in-presentation questions include:

- So, what can we do?
- What does established research tell us?
- What can we learn from this?

Questions: replying to audience comments

This is the part of a presentation which many presenters dread – questions from the audience. The key to dealing with questions is research. Hopefully you will know enough about your subject but you should do some thinking about your audience – are they academic, industrial or a mix of the two? Put yourself in their shoes – which questions would you ask?

> *"I can't see the people out front. The lights cover them after the first three or four rows. But I feel them, I hear them... if you see an attractive chick down there and you start doing the show for her, then you lose everybody else"*
>
> ***Sammy Davis Junior, "Why Me?", Michael Joseph: London, 1989***

With careful research on your part, you should be able to anticipate questions so they do not come as any great surprise to you. You should encourage questions as honestly as you can. As mentioned earlier, do not start to pack up your papers as you ask, "Any questions"? This serves either to deter questions or, worse, antagonise questioners so that they proceed to grill you.

When is the best time to take questions?

This is a matter of personal preference. Sometimes, your supervisors will tell you whether questions are to take place after completion of your presentation.

Some presenters like to allow questions as they proceed through the presentation as this can clear up any confusion that the audience may have. They are less likely to be antagonistic to you at the end of the presentation. The downside with handling questions during the presentation is that you may get side-tracked so that you lose focus, forget where you were or repeat yourself; to the audience, this will not look good.

Anticipating questions

Being in control of your presentation involves some anticipation of questions at the end of your presentation. As you have written the presentation (and hence should know it inside out), you should be in full control of answering questions that arise.

Although it may be difficult, try to put yourself in your audience's position: if you had just sat through your presentation, what would your questions be? Go through your presentation on a slide-by-slide basis and note down any questions (and, of course, associated answers) **that you have yourself about the slide.**

If you are particularly nervous about the presentation, noting down your own questions (and answers) onto index cards can be very useful to calm nerves. Before the presentation, quickly reading through these index cards is a useful way to calm nerves and focus your mind.

Body language can be important when asking the audience if there are any questions. As mentioned earlier, do not pack up your things as you ask the audience; not only is this rude, it is less likely that they will ask you anything (if you are being assessed on your question handling ability, you may lose marks).

Listen to the question

When someone asks you a question, have the courtesy to look directly at them (without eyeballing them, though). Looking at the questioner shows that you have respect for them but do not interrupt them while they ask the question. Wait until you've heard the entire question before answering. By interrupting, you run the risk of embarrassing both yourself and the questioner if you mis-hear or misunderstand the question.

Repeat the question

It is good practice to repeat the question. By doing so, other audience members who perhaps did not hear the question the first time are now clear. Secondly, this gives you a few valuable seconds in which to formulate a clear and concise reply.

If the question is vague, use this opportunity to rephrase the question in a clearer manner. Do not be afraid to ask for clarification if it is required. The worst thing you can do is to give a brilliant answer to a question that simply was not asked.

Above all, do not get defensive. As part of your preparation regarding question anticipation, try to empathise with the audience. By putting yourself into their shoes, you are more likely to empathise with their position, their background and therefore their motivation for asking the question.

Speed of reply

Some students fall into the trap of thinking that the quicker they answer, the more the audience will like it. This is not always true. By taking some time to reflect on the questioner to formulate your answer, this conveys to the audience that you are thinking about the question and that you are treating it, and therefore the questioner, with respect.

There is, however, a middle ground to aim for. Do not pause for too long as this suggests that either you do not understand the question (in which case you should ask for clarification) or you do not know the answer. If the latter, do not be afraid to ask the questioner to rephrase the question. Alternatively, rephrase the question yourself and ask: "is this what you are asking?"

When answering the question, do not simply re-read a line from your presentation. The questioner is asking for further detail (merely re-reading a line from your presentation will not help to answer a question that may not have been asked if the line had been clearer in the first place).

Finally, remember that you should look at the questioner as they ask the question, but that you should look at everybody in the audience when you reply – although the question is for you, the answer is for everyone.

What if there are no questions?

If you are faced with the (unlikely) scenario where the audience members do not have any questions for you, you may have to kick start things by asking something like: "Well, when I was researching this presentation, one of the things I asked myself was..." and then ask a question. Have at least one question like this prepared in case the audience does not ask you anything.

> ***"There's no answer to that."***
>
> ***Eric Morecambe, comedian***

TIPS: Replying to questions

TIP 1 **Active listening** – pay careful attention to the questioner and the question in its entirety (do not interrupt the questioner). Waiting until you hear the full question buys you valuable seconds in which to formulate a more directed reply.

TIP 2 **Repeat the question** – skilled presenters tend to repeat the question which has just been asked for a variety of reasons including:

(a) to ensure that they have heard the question correctly;

(b) for the benefit of others in the room who may not have heard the question clearly; and

(c) to buy the presenters a few valuable seconds to focus their reply.

TIP 3 **Rephrase the question** – if the questioner has asked a potentially confusing question, you can rephrase the question better for the benefit of the audience, enabling you to provide a more focussed answer

TIP 4 **Look at the questioner** – without eyeballing them of course! This enables you to forge a short, yet intimate, relationship with the questioner (remember though to occasionally look at other members of the audience but always return your eyes to the original questioner).

TIP 5 **Thank all the questioners** – as a simple matter of courtesy, thank the audience for their time, their attention and their questions.

Remember that the question-and-answer session should only be a small proportion of the full presentation. There may be a temptation to:

Talk too much... Try to keep your answers to the point but, above all, brief. The audience will not want to hear a long, drawn-out answer – they have just sat through your presentation remember. Their questions should be for clarification or further explanation if necessary. Additionally, if you talk too much, the audience may be deterred from asking further questions.

Interrupt... You run the risk of appearing arrogant or, worse still, you may embarrass yourself if your anticipation is wrong.

Ramble... If you think that the question will take too long to answer, answer it as best you can in brief but then invite the questioner to talk with you more after the presentation (note that this is not possible in, say, an academic project presentation – in this case, answer as briefly as you can)

Lie... You will be found out! It is always best to admit that you don't know but will try to find out and contact the questioner afterwards.

Checklist

In this chapter, we have:

- looked at how best to capture and retain your audience's attention
- discussed the importance of a strong and clear voice
- acknowledged the use of good eye contact and stage movement
- examined how to encourage and answer audience questions.

Chapter 5

CHECKLISTS AND FINAL TIPS

Chapter summary

This chapter will assimilate and present several checklists which can be used as a basis for final preparations for your presentation. Several vignettes and anecdotes from former students and academic tutors are presented.

Learning outcomes

After studying this chapter, you should be able to do the following:

Outcome 1: look at the provided checklists and use them as a basis for final preparation or as an *aide memoire*.

Outcome 2: gain insights from the experiences of both former students and academic tutors.

The aim of this chapter is to present key ideas which can be used as a simple aide memoire as you make your final preparations for your presentation.

We also present a simple checklist to help you reflect back on the presentation (i.e. once you have done it). By looking back and remembering the presentation, you will be able to appraise and evaluate:

- what went well;
- what went badly;
- how to present yourself better for your next presentation.

It should be noted that your own reflections and memories should be used in conjunction with the opinions, marks and comments of your audience.

☑ Checklist 1: Research

- What is the purpose of your presentation?
- What are the boundaries / how far can you go / what is your remit?
- How much time do you have?
- How much can you realistically get across to your audience in this time?
- Is there a prescribed format or style?
- Do you know the composition of your audience?
- Are they familiar with your topic?
- Can you perhaps anticipate their biases and questions?
- Is your presentation geared appropriately towards your audience?
- Have you taken a look at the room?
- Can you influence seating / screen, etc.?
- What type of equipment is provided?
- Is it in good working order?
- Can you control lighting, temperature, windows and so forth?

☑ Checklist 3: Presentation Delivery

BEGINNING

- Be positive and remember to smile.
- What is the presentation about (title slide)?
- What are your aims and objectives?
- Introduce yourself! (Name, details on title slide too.)
- Grab their attention.
- Say a little about the background and context.
- What will the audience gain by hearing what you have to say?
- Include an agenda slide (set the scene).
- Be in control – say when you expect to finish, when you prefer to take questions (during or after).
- Are there handouts? When are you giving these out?

MIDDLE

- In the main body, remember to tell the audience about your context and problem in detail.
- Is this in an order that flows (logical)?
- Are you clear and concise?
- Are you using a language that they will understand? (For a technical project, appraise your audience...using an overtly technical language to a non-technical audience will either lose or confuse them; explaining these terms to a technical audience may insult their intelligence! Aim for the middle ground.)
- Give them detail where required.
- Vignettes and anecdotes can add colour to your point.
- How is this relevant to them? What can they learn?

END

- Remember to close well!
- Have a summary or conclusion slide prepared.
- Go over the most important points of your presentation.
- What were the benefits of your approach?
- Are there any further recommendations?
- Positively invite questions... remember to listen carefully to the questioner ...and remember to answer the question!

☑ Checklist 4: Keeping Audience Interest

- Remember that YOU are in control of the presentation.
- Smile (we have already said this, but is worth mentioning again).
- Try to check audience body language to check for bored members or signs of not understanding, etc.
- Check your own body language as well!
- Don't READ from a script (although "cheat sheets" – index cards, etc. are fine).
- Keep good eye contact (although don't eyeball anyone).
- Hands and arms can be used for emphasis.
- Be clear and concise.
- Be enthusiastic.
- Voice: be loud enough to be heard.
- Voice: vary pace for emphasis.
- Voice: use pauses for effect.
- Start strong, continue strong, finish strong!

☑ Checklist 5: Miscellaneous

- Practice makes perfect.
- Remember to rehearse your presentation.
- Check your material.
- Check the available equipment.
- Try to check out the room, layout, equipment, etc. beforehand.
- Have a drink of water to hand in case you get "dry mouth".
- Get a good night's sleep.
- Try to enjoy the experience.

☑ Checklist 6: Reflection (After Your Presentation)

In order to iron out wrinkles for your next presentation, think back to your presentation and consider the following:

- How was your content?
- How was your style?
- How did you cope with audience questions?
- How was your time management?
- How do you think the audience reacted?
- What areas can you improve?
- Get feedback, informal and formal from tutors if you can.

Final viewpoint...

Many former students and academic tutors/supervisors were kind enough to contribute words of advice and hints which are present throughout the text. Some were so detailed that we were unable to reproduce them by way of insert boxes but they offered such insight that we are happy to present them below in the form of anecdotes and vignettes.

...from students

"Keep your eye contact with every member of your audience; it helps to gain back your self-confidence. Use simple language; avoid memorising your speech or any words. Never read from notes, even if you think you will miss some important points, practice more."

Ameneh Mojtabai,
former student

"In my first year at university, part of our coursework for a marketing module was to get into groups and sell our tutor a mortgage. I was in a group with a very nervous presenter who wasn't that well prepared. Throughout the whole presentation he sat and chewed gum very loudly. When it was his turn to speak, he pretty much hid behind his piece of paper which had his notes on and rattled through his piece at 1000 words a minute whilst still chewing his gum. Needless to say we didn't manage to sell our mortgage...

...When I am nervous during a presentation I tend to shuffle, tap my feet, rock from side to side and generally fidget. I didn't realise this until on a presentation skills course when my tutor pointed out the fidgeting.

Over the next couple of hours, we practised presenting to large and small groups and, on almost every occasion, I'd fidget. The next day my tutor brought in a large sheet of greaseproof paper and made me stand on it whenever I was presenting. Everytime I began to shuffle, rock or tap my feet, the greaseproof paper would rustle and remind me to keep my b***** feet still!"

Laura Harrison,
former student

"If you are using a presentation package such as PowerPoint®, try to test your presentation well in advance on the computer it will actually be running on. Occasionally there will be technology incompatibilities (versions of PowerPoint®, fonts, presence of QuickTime) that need to be resolved before your presentation will run. There's nothing more horrifying after having spent hours perfecting a presentation, than to turn up 30 minutes before you are due to go on stage, only to discover your presentation files don't work as expected...

... Always speak more slowly than you think you are. Nerves can cause you to waffle and race without realising it. Slow down...

When on stage, keep the 'rules of the game' in the back of your mind, but remember above all to enjoy the moment. When all is said and done, there's nothing more captivating to an audience than seeing someone who's genuinely interested in the subject they're talking about."

Tim Thompson,
former student

"See anxiety as a positive factor, it will force you to be better prepared...

...pay attention on your appearance, definitely you do not want the audience to be absorbed by the Mickey Mouse tie that you wear...

...the variation of your voice and expression, the absence of negative words in your speech, but also your sense of humour are vital points for a good presentation."

Paris Parissis,
former student

...from academics

"The coursework assignment for this final year undergraduate module was for students to form groups of about four, and then to be responsible for running a seminar, with the intention of offering a learning opportunity for the class. Two of the prime assessment criteria were:

1.The quality of the learning opportunity for the class.

2.The management of the whole seminar, in every respect.

Most students included at least 20 minutes of formal presentation at the beginning of the class using PowerPoint®, then broke out into small group activities. However, there was one group, who had not attended much throughout the year, who were one of the final groups to complete the assessment. Both students and tutor were becoming restless when there was no sign of the group 10 minutes after the start of class. As the seminar was about to break up assuming the group weren't going to show up, one member of the group rushed in, saying that the others were on their way.

He brandished his disk, on which the presentation purportedly resided, asking where the laptop was, and showed much astonishment when he found out his group were supposed to arrange to provide their own, or borrow one from the School Technical Department. The tutor had a laptop, which he agreed to set up for them, which used up more scarce time. The other members of the group arrived (they had apparently been in the computer lab downstairs finishing their PowerPoint® presentation). Unfortunately when the disk was inserted the file refused to open. The students were in such a rush to finish in the lab they removed the disk before it had finished saving. Back downstairs they went to try to rescue the file, and returned five minutes later with a working presentation.

By the time they started, the students had less than 25 minutes in which to complete the class. The presentation itself was poor, with the speakers rushed and flustered. The content was not appropriate for the level of study, and the class gained little from the whole episode. The group comprehensively failed the assignment.

Technical equipment, room layout and preparation will not of themselves gain you a high mark. But lack of preparation, and especially a failure to develop contingency plans to accommodate failure in some facilitating feature or equipment can have disproportionate or disastrous consequences."

Dr Gerald Unwin,
Coventry Business School, Coventry University

...from the authors

We hope that this book has been:

- useful for novice (and perhaps nervous) presenters;
- useful for more experienced presenters in order to refine their presentation practice.

Remember that presentations are an essential skill in the commercial sector. Getting things right during your time at university or college allows you to gain valuable feedback from experienced tutors so that, when you embark on your industrial careers, you know what to expect, are not nervous and, above all, can act professionally.

Checklist

In this chapter, we have:

- presented several checklists for final preparations;
- provided vignettes which illustrate academic experiences, from the viewpoint of both students and staff.

Appendix

MICROSOFT POWERPOINT 2003 IN A NUTSHELL

This appendix describes how to use PowerPoint, a powerful presentation software program from the Microsoft Office 2003 software suite.

A Microsoft PowerPoint presentation is called a slideshow.

A suite is a group of programs designed by a single manufacturer (in this case Microsoft) that work well together.

Using PowerPoint, you can create a basic customised slideshow (i.e. a presentation).

Because Microsoft PowerPoint 2003 is an integral component of the Microsoft Office suite of products, PowerPoint is very similar to Office applications, such as Microsoft Word or Microsoft Excel. Furthermore, you can very easily reuse the work that you have done in Microsoft Word or Microsoft Excel.

For example, if you have created a graph in Microsoft Excel, you can use that graph on a Microsoft PowerPoint slide and vice versa (i.e. one could copy text, tables, and graphics from a PowerPoint presentation and export them to Microsoft Word or Microsoft Excel).

Getting started with Microsoft PowerPoint 2003

To start PowerPoint, click the **Start** button, then Click **All Programs** in case of Windows XP or **Programs** in case of Windows 2000, then click **Microsoft Office, followed by Microsoft Office PowerPoint 2003** (*see Figure 1*).

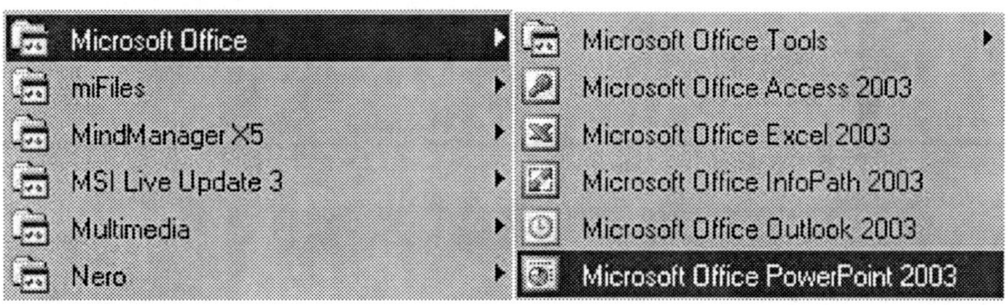

Figure 1

If your Windows desktop includes a PowerPoint shortcut icon (*see Figure 2*), you can use it to start the program. Simply double-click the icon to open the program.

Figure 2

The PowerPoint program will open and will look very much like the opening screen shown in *Figure 3*. Your screen might differ slightly depending on the options that you chose during installation.

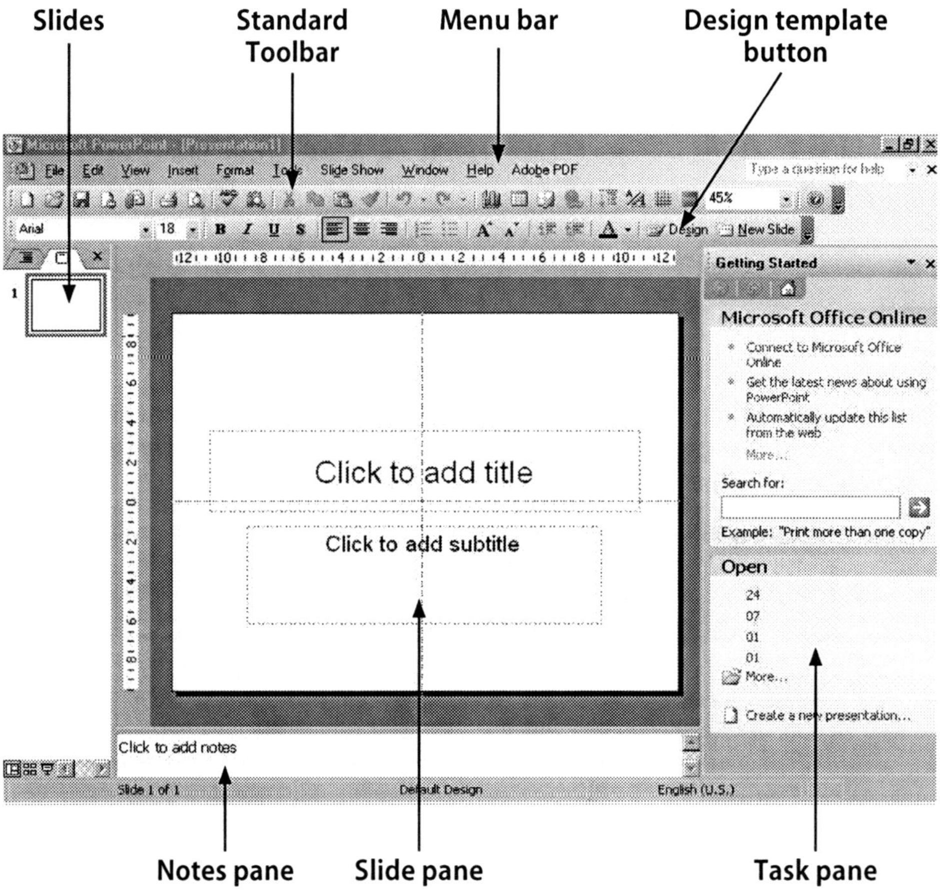

Figure 3: The opening screen

Menu bar

The **menu bar** is used to perform specific actions (i.e. to create a new presentation, save a presentation, etc.). The default menu bar includes nine menu categories, each displaying a list of related commands. *Figure 3* shows the default nine menu bar categories and an additional menu bar category entitled Adobe PDF.

Toolbar

A toolbar is similar to a menu, in the sense that it is a graphical representation of a series of related commands for executing similar tasks. The first three buttons (from the extreme left-hand side of *Figure 3*) allow a user to create a new presentation, open an existing presentation and save a presentation. In *Figure 3*, the **Standard** and **Formatting** toolbars appear at the top. This is the default option.

You can display toolbars by right-clicking any visible toolbar (in this case either the **Standard** toolbar or the **Formatting** toolbar) and choosing from the desired toolbar listed in the sub-menu.

Task pane

This pane is displayed automatically when you start PowerPoint. It offers you the option of creating a new presentation and also provides links for the last few presentations that you have worked on. You have the option of closing the **Task pane** (which is a good thing to do, especially if you are working on a 15 or a 17-inch monitor). Closing the **Task pane** allows you to gain more room to work on the individual presentation slides that appear in the centre of the screen (i.e. in the **Slide pane**).

Slide pane

This is the most widely used pane as you this is where you will work on the slides for your presentation. You can also customise this pane to display two or more slides.

Notes pane

You can use the **Notes pane** to add speaker notes about each slide. This allows you to present important information associated with each slide. This option is especially useful if you are preparing a presentation for somebody else.

Creating a presentation

PowerPoint offers you four very different ways of creating a presentation (depending on the amount of content and design assistance desired). You can create:

1 **A presentation using the AutoContent Wizard:** The **AutoContent Wizard** is an automated way of creating a presentation. It guides the user via a step-by-step process to creating a presentation. Of the four different ways

of creating a presentation, the **AutoContent Wizard** offers the novice user the maximum assistance. The user has to answer a few basic questions about the presentation desired and PowerPoint does the rest. The downside of the method is that the user has no control over the design slide template and the slide layout that is applied to the presentation. The **AutoContent Wizard** is an easy way to make a presentation, especially if you are in a hurry, are not design savvy (see points discussed later about the design slide template and the slide layout) and are not sure how to present your ideas.

2 **A presentation using a design template:** A design template allows the user to create a new presentation using a preformatted template. The user can select a design template from numerous possibilities, all of which are automatically installed when PowerPoint is set up on your system. The advantage of this approach is that you can add slides (one at a time) and all would share the scheme (i.e. the same look and feel).

   You should use the design template to create a new presentation, especially if you have used PowerPoint a few times before. The presentation prepared with an appropriate design template goes a long way in ensuring that the final presentation appears professional.

3 **A blank presentation:** As the title suggests, a blank presentation is, to put it simply – a very basic presentation. The presentation is just black text on a white background. The user is offered no content and design suggestions. You should use this method of creating a new presentation if you are very experienced with PowerPoint and would also like to create a customised presentation (i.e. slide design and layout).

4 **A new presentation using an existing presentation:** Another way to create a new presentation is simply to copy an existing presentation whose content and format are similar to the presentation that you would to create. The advantage of using this option is that you can create a presentation by copying another one and then editing the text. When you copy a presentation, you are copying the slide design, the slide layout and all the slides.

The AutoContent Wizard

To create a presentation using the **AutoContent Wizard**, follow these steps:

Select **File**, and then **New** (*see Figure 4*) to display the **New Presentation task pane** if it isn't already shown (*see Figure 5*).

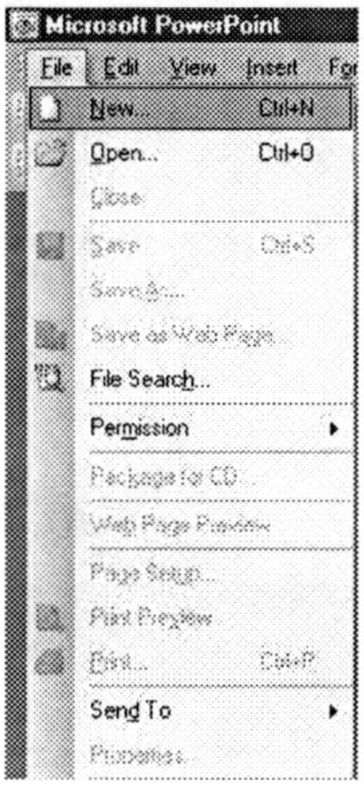

Figure 4

In the **Task pane**, click **From AutoContent Wizard** (*see Figure 5*).

Figure 5

The **AutoContent Wizard** will open:

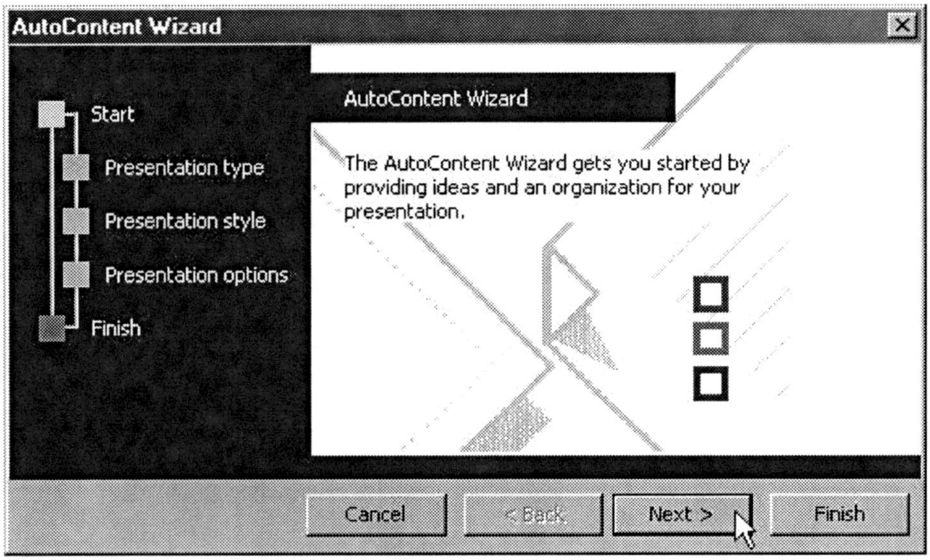

Figure 6

Click **Next** to continue (*see Figure 6*).

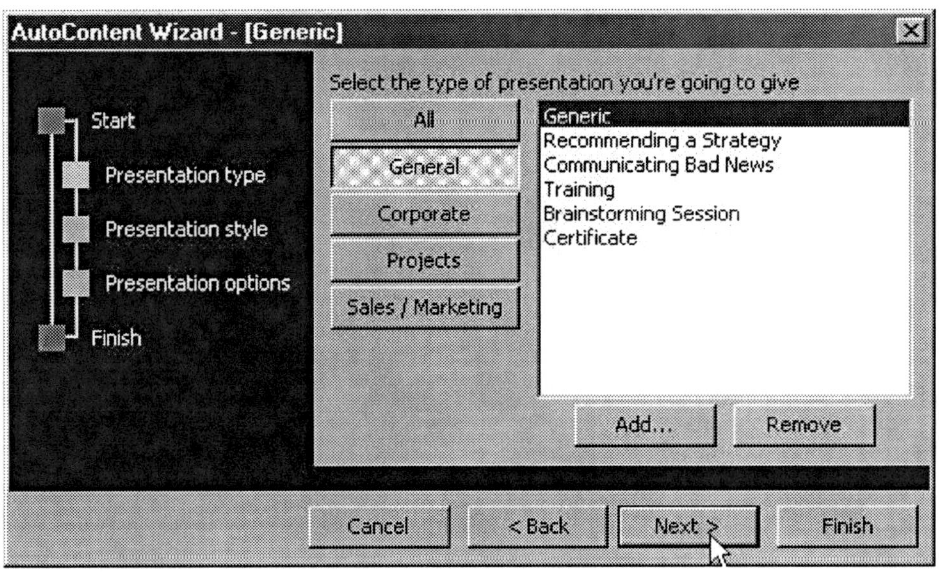

Figure 7

This screen (*see Figure 7*), lists different types of presentation. Each type of presentation is further divided into a number of categories. You must select a type and category similar to your presentation concept and then modify the slides to suit your own needs. In this case the **General** type of presentation and a **Generic** category has been selected.

Click **Next** to continue.

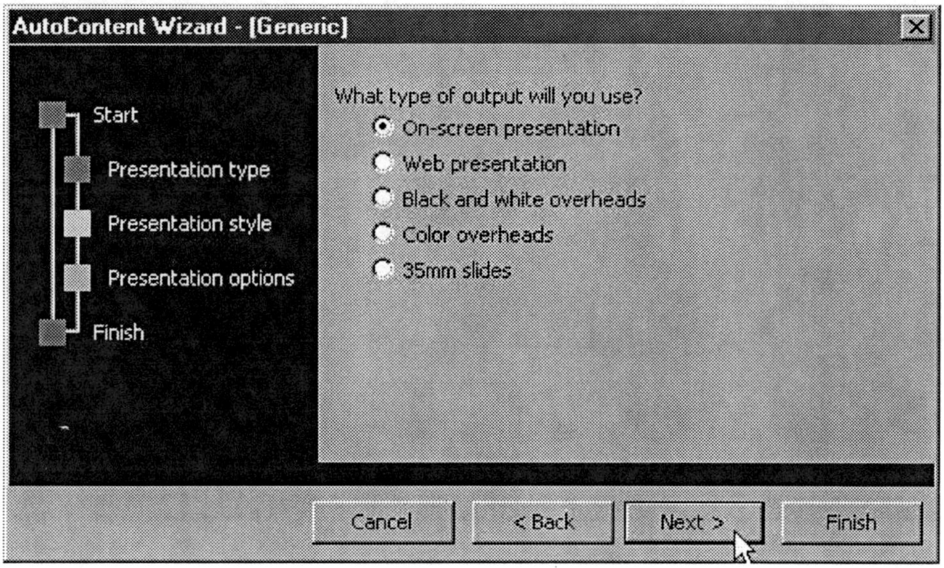

Figure 8

Select the type of method that best describes how you want to give your presentation, and then click **Next** to continue. In this case (*see Figure 8*), the **On-screen presentation** mode has been selected.

- **Onscreen presentation:** This is the standard presentation format, delivered on a computer screen.
- **Web presentation:** This format is used to deliver presentations via the web/Internet.
- **Black-and-white overheads:** This format is generally used to produce a cost-effective alternative to full-colour transparencies.
- **Colour overheads:** This format is usually used to produce full-colour transparencies.
- **35mm slides:** This format is generally used to create transparencies that are formatted for delivery to allow conversion to 35mm slides (you would have to take the file to a professional graphics agency, which would produce the 35mm slides).

Type a title for the presentation (i.e. "Audience Interest" – *see Figure 9*). The title appears on the first slide in the presentation. Optionally, you can also type in any footer text you'd like to appear at the bottom of each slide.

By default, the **AutoContent Wizard** includes the date and slide number at the bottom of each slide. In this case, we decided to turn off these features. This was done by deselecting the check boxes (*see Figure 9*).

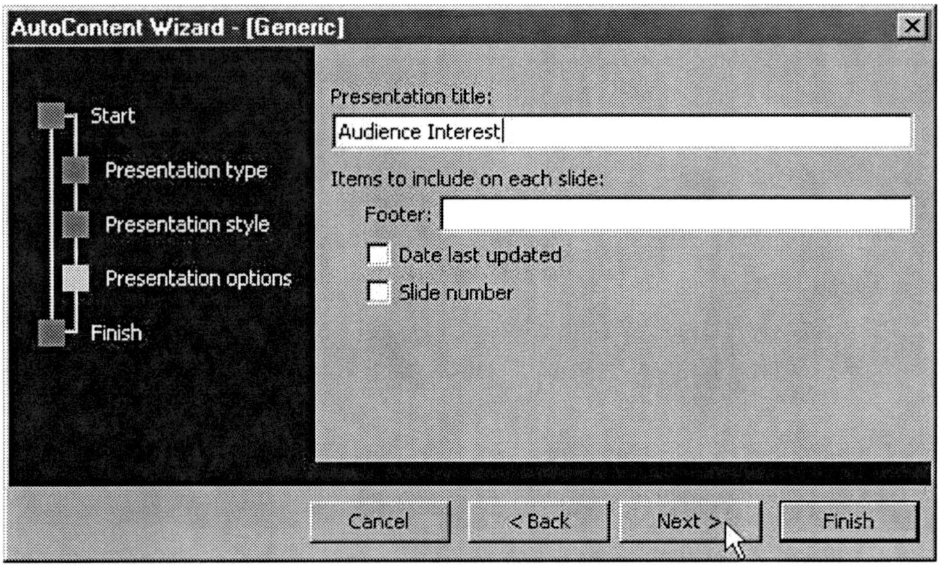

Figure 9

Click **Next** to continue.

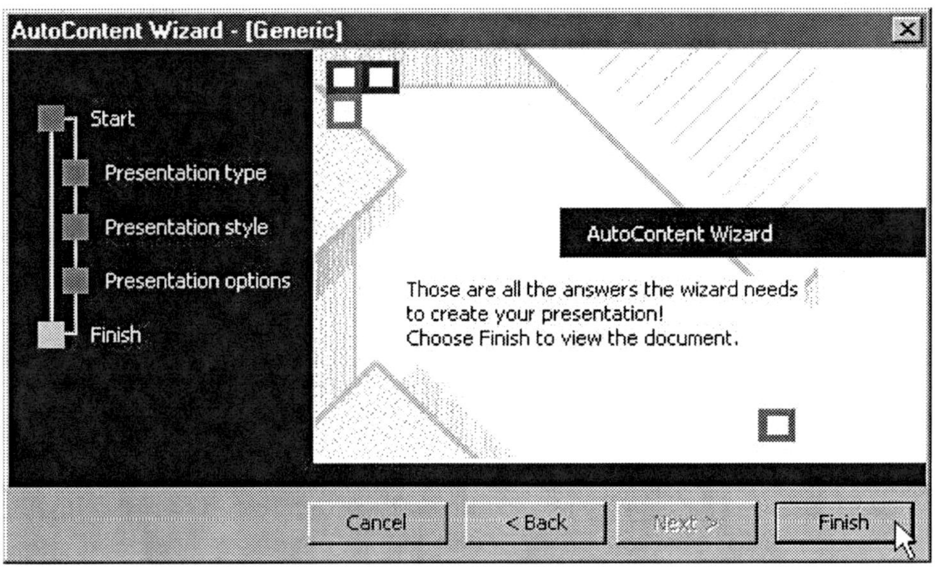

Figure 10

After you complete the **AutoContent Wizard's** steps, click **Finish**. the wizard generates a sample presentation that matches the style you requested (*see Figure 11*).

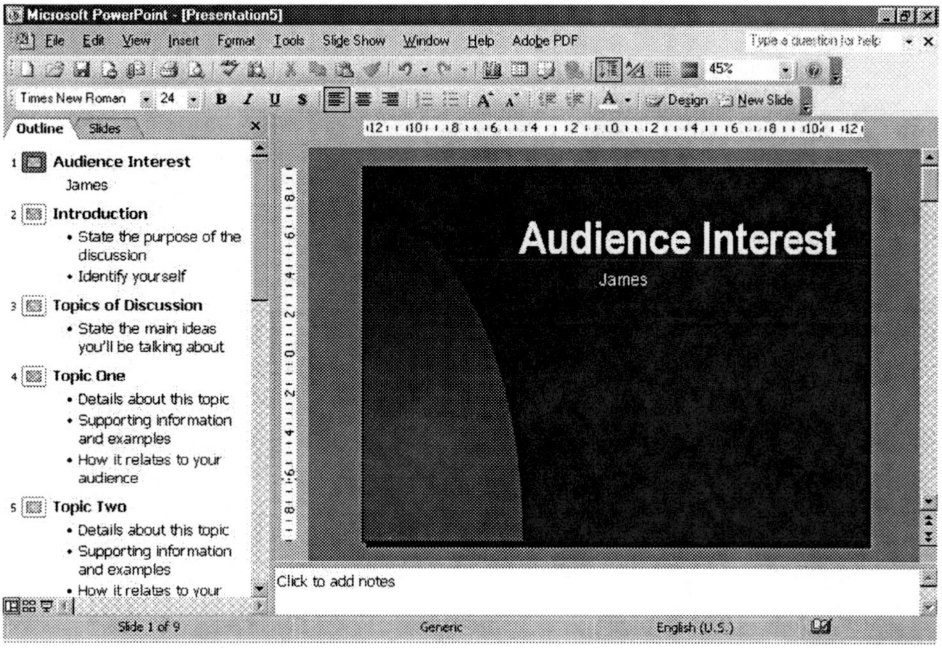

Figure 11

The text on each slide (including the title slide) is preformatted, so all you have to do is add your own text. In this case (*see Figure 11*), PowerPoint automatically adds the user name (in this case James). PowerPoint does this by inserting the document owner's name from the document's properties.

You can also select any slide you want to modify by **clicking** on the **slide number** in the **Slide Outline pane** (*see Figure 12*). In this case, we moved to slide 2 by clicking on slide number 2 in the **Slide Outline pane**.

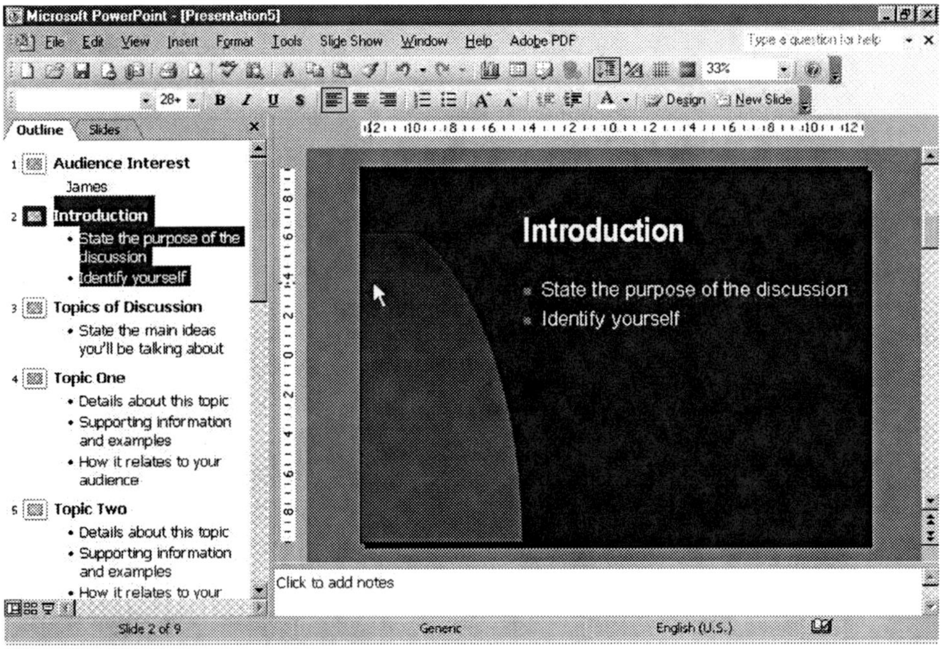

Figure 12

Saving the presentation

Once you have finished working on your presentation, remember to save it. PowerPoint 2003 allows you save a presentation in a variety of ways, including as:

- a regular **Presentation**, readable by PowerPoint 2003, or choose from the other options so that the presentation can be opened in earlier versions (2002, 2000, 97, and 95);
- a **Web page**, as a folder or a **Web archive** as a single file;
- a **Design Template**, so that you can create presentations based upon your own customised layout;
- a **PowerPoint show**, ready to run on its own and will run on other PCs that don't have a full version of PowerPoint installed. The PC will, however, require **PowerPoint Viewer** to be installed, available for **www.microsoft.com**.
- a **graphic image**.

At this stage, we will save our work as a regular presentation. To do so, we will follow the following steps:

- Click the **File** menu and then the **Save** menu item (*see Figure 13*).

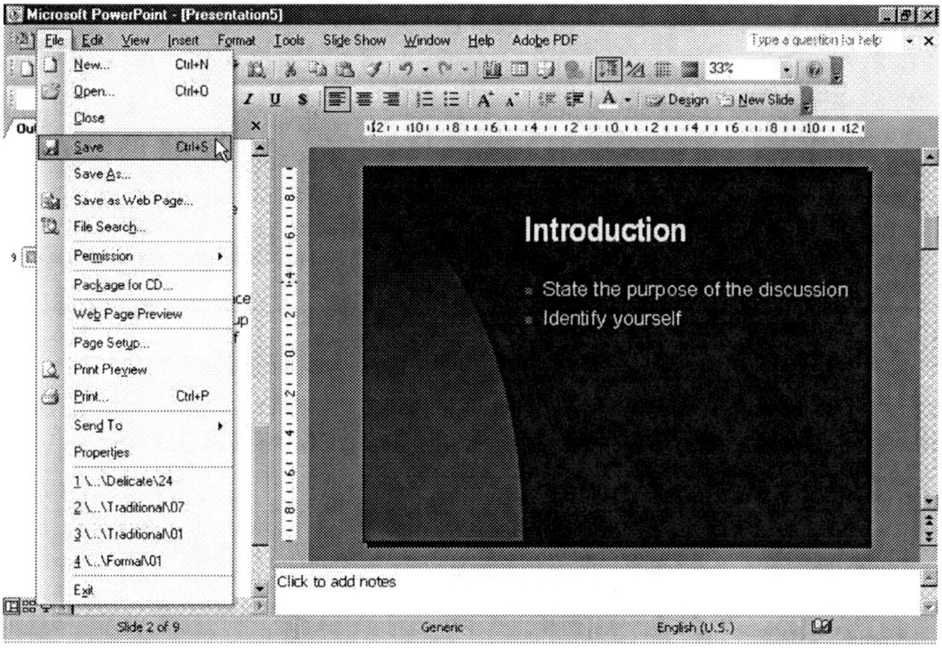

Figure 13

- The **Save As** dialog box opens. Type a name for the presentation. The title of the slide is selected as the default filename (which you may change to suite your needs) and also offers to save this file in the **My Documents** folder. In this case (*see Figure 14*), we accept these two choices and click **Save.**

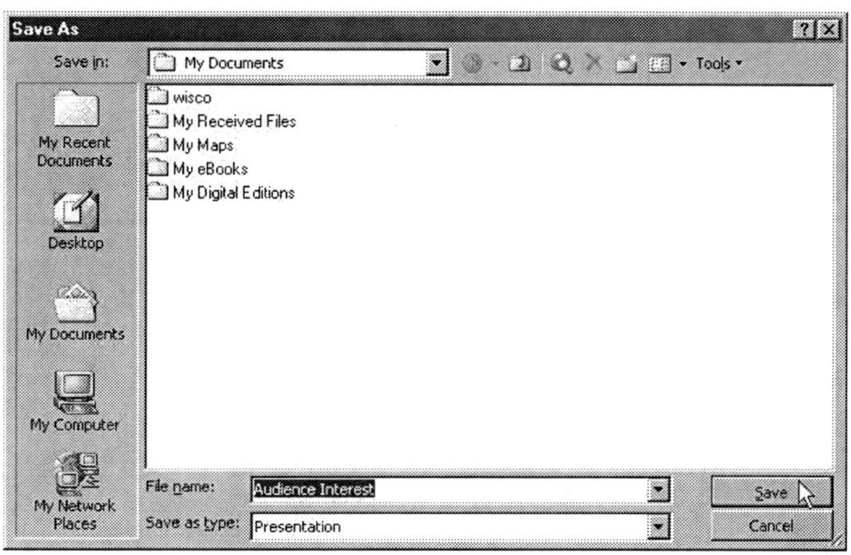

Figure 14

Creating a presentation using a design template

You can also create a presentation from one of the predefined presentation design templates provided with PowerPoint.

TIP

A design template is simply a preformatted template with specific colour schemes, font styles, and background. Some organisations, such as universities and businesses have their own custom templates to ensure that all presentations represent a specific "corporate image".

To create a presentation using a design template, follow these steps:

Select **File**, and then **New** (*see Figure 4*) to display the **New Presentation task pane** if it isn't already displayed. Click **From Design Template** (*see Figure 15*).

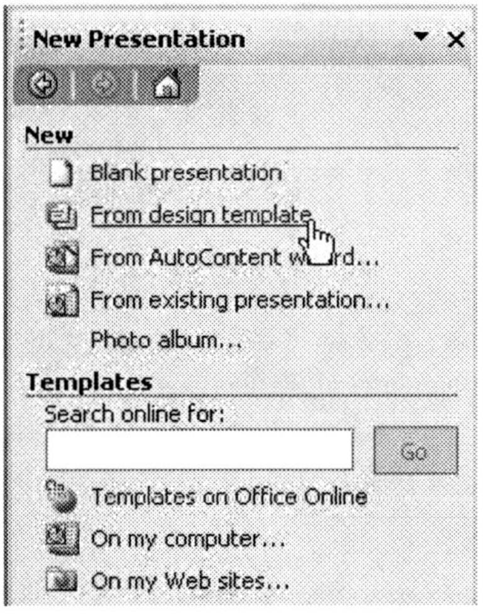

Figure 15

TIP

You can download free design templates from the Microsoft website. To do this, scroll to the bottom of the **Slide Design pane** and then click on **Templates on Office Online**. You will be directed to the design template site at **www.microsoft.com**. You have to be connected to the Internet to download design templates.

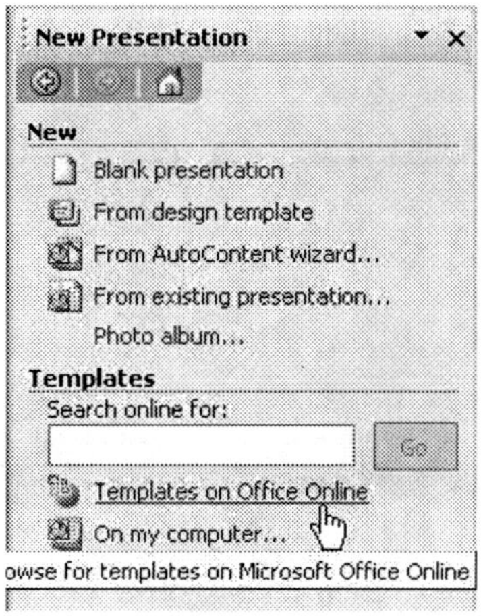

Figure 16

Once you select **Click From Design Template,** as shown in *Figure 15*, the **Slide Design pane** opens (*see Figure 17*). You have the opportunity to review a number of design templates and select the design template you feel is appropriate for your presentation.

In *Figure 17*, we have selected the design template named **Layers**. Each new slide that we add to our presentation will share the same common design (i.e. the look and feel of all the slides will be the same).

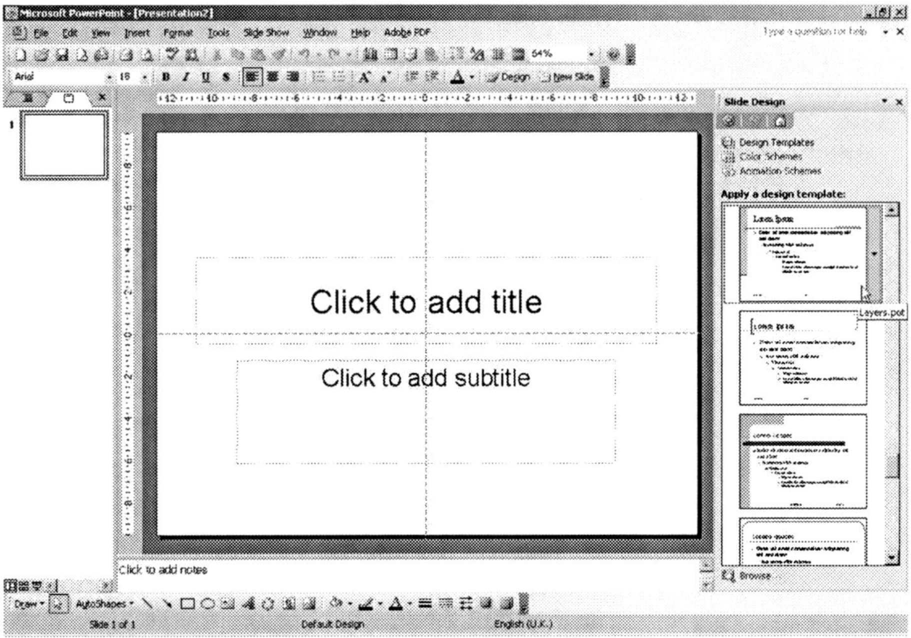

Figure 17

To add a new slide in a PowerPoint presentation

To add a new slide, select **Insert,** and then select **New Slide** (*see Figure 18*). You can do the same by pressing the **Ctrl + M** keys on the keyboard simultaneously.

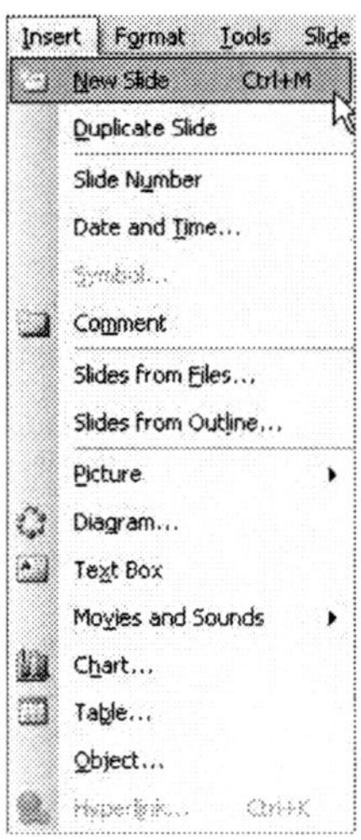

Figure 18

TIP

If you do not like the design you have selected, you can choose another, or click the Undo button located on the Standard toolbar to return to the previous design.

Another advantage of using design templates is that you can customise each slide using slide layouts. The default slide layout is a title and text layout (an example of which can be seen in *Figure 19*). Most presentations will require slides that combine pictures, tables and text in one slide and each slide may be different from others in terms of its content requirements (i.e. text, tables, charts and pictures).

Furthermore, if you do not like the current slide's layout, you can use the **Slide Layout pane** to select a new one. In our example (*see Figure 19*), we are going to change the default title and text layout to title and a two-column text layout.

To change the current slide layout combination

To change the current slide layout combination, simply click the desired layout in **Slide Layout** in the **Task pane** (*see Figure 19*).

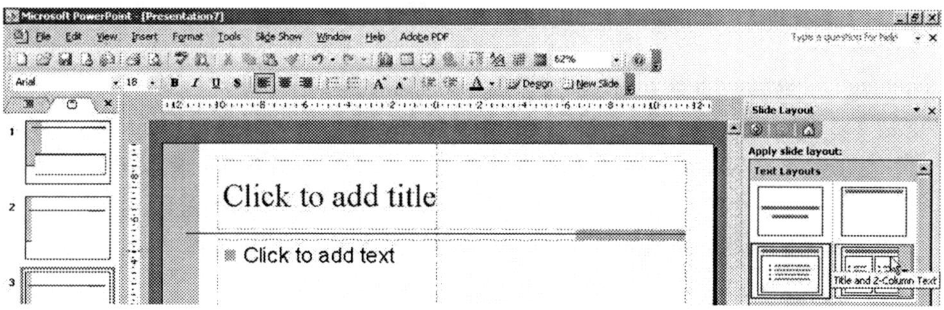

Figure 19

Once you click the desired slide layout, the current slide will automatically be modified. In our example, the layout (*see Figure 19*) has been modified to a two-column text layout (*see Figure 20*).

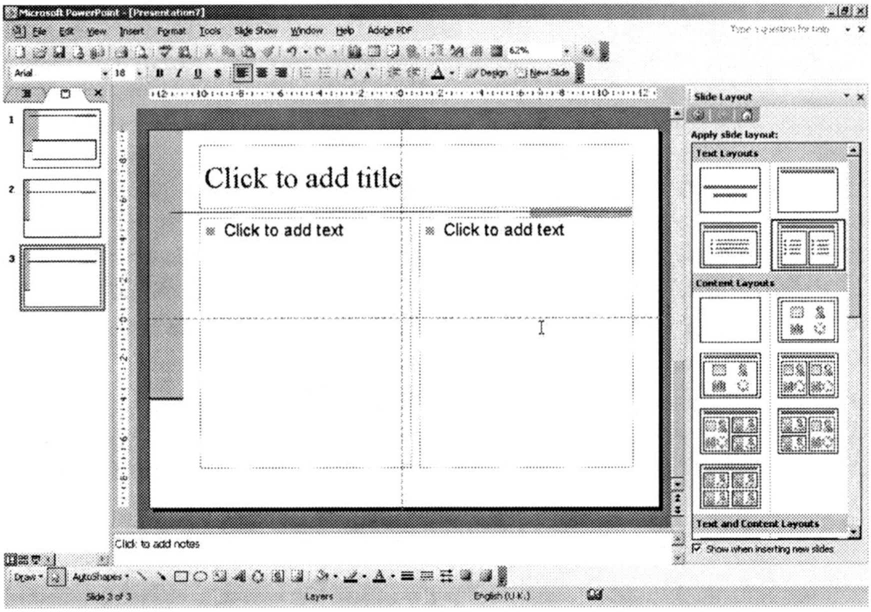

Figure 20

To add a chart to your PowerPoint presentation

To add a chart to your slide, click on the **Content** tab, which is located on the right-hand side of the **Slide Layout pane**, under the **Content Layouts** header (*see Figure 21*).

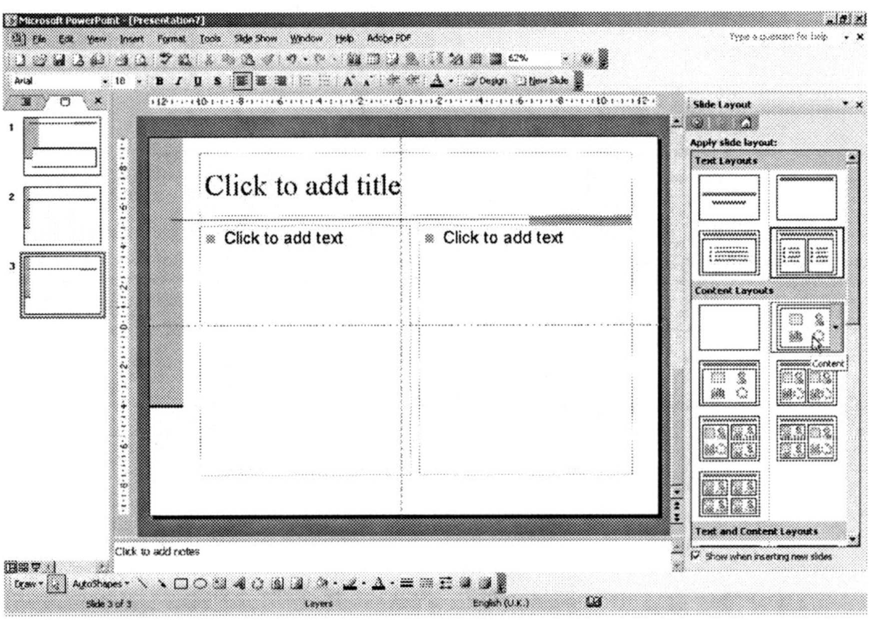

Figure 21

Once you click on the **Content** tab, the following screen will appear:

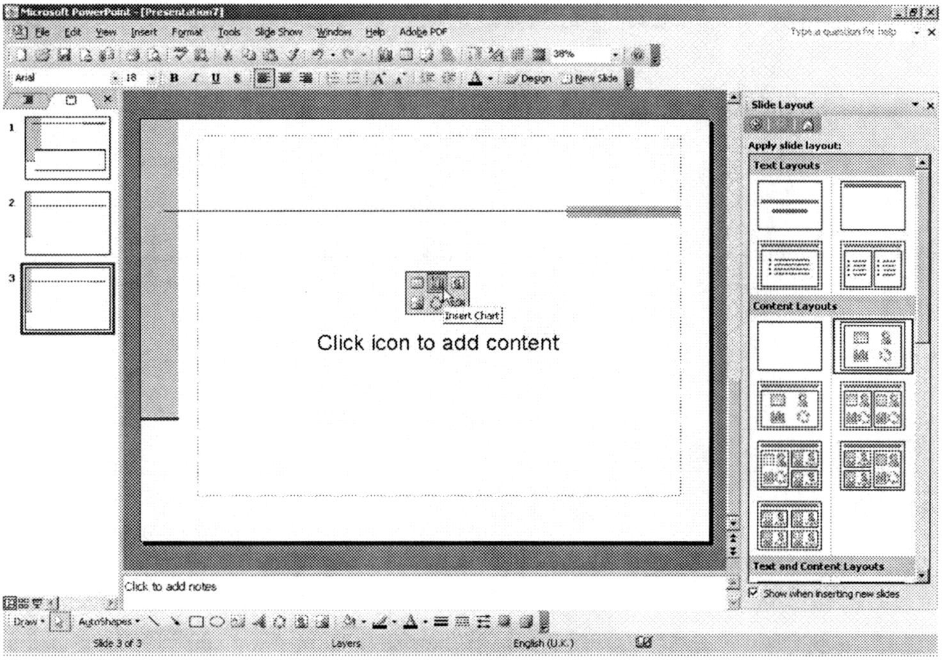

Figure 22

To insert a chart click the **Insert Chart** button (*see Figure 23*).

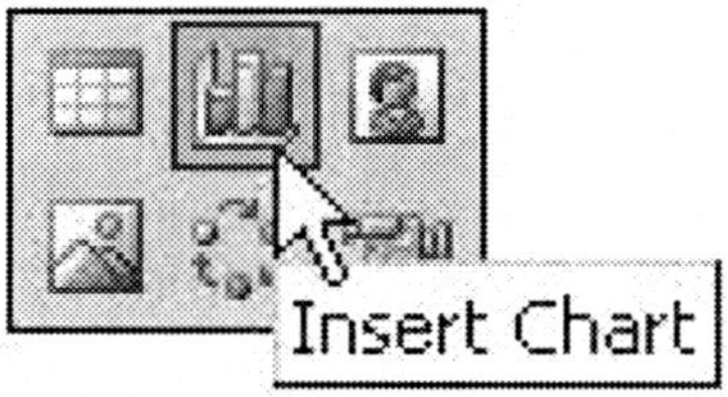

Figure 23

PowerPoint will automatically use **Microsoft Graph** to create a chart. *Figure 24* shows what will be displayed after you click the **Insert Chart** button. The default chart display is a sample 3D clustered column chart. Along with the chart, the datasheet will also appear (*see Figure 24*). You can modify both the data and the chart type using the specially customised Microsoft Graph's menu bar.

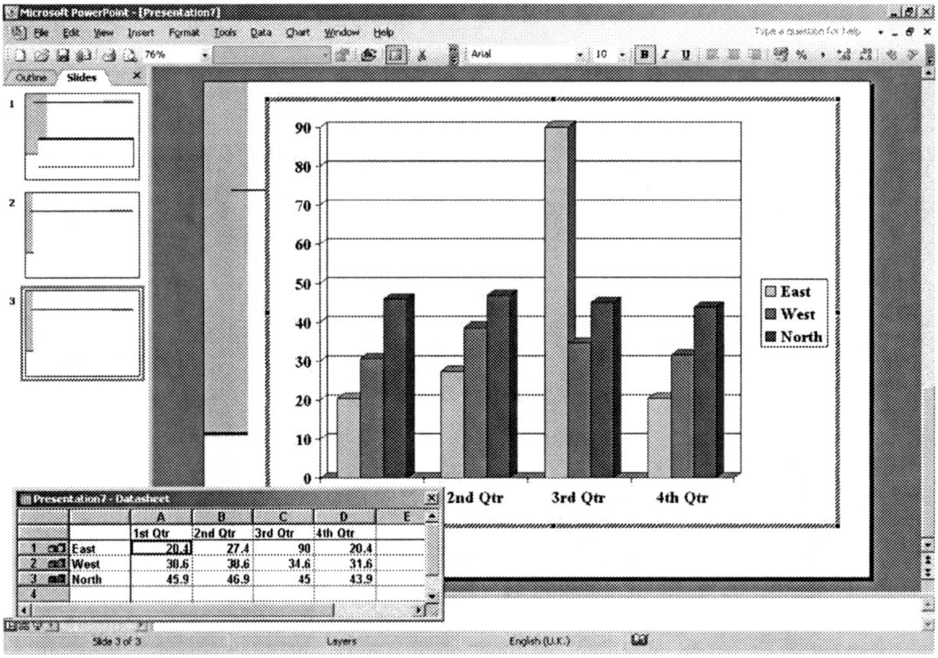

Figure 24

To modify the data and the chart you would have to use the **Data** and **Chart** menu items located in the **menu bar**. For example, to create a diagram for the following table, you would have to delete one column from the datasheet in *Figure 24.*

	2003	**2004**	**2005**
Coventry	12000	14000	15400
Hull	12500	13500	14800
York	15000	16000	17000

Table 1: Number of students enrolled at three UK universities from 2003 to 2005

If we compare the datasheet as depicted in *Figure 24* with Table 1, we can see that both Figure 24 and Table 1 each have three rows of data, but *Figure 24* has four columns whilst Table 1 has only three columns. Therefore we can delete one column from the datasheet in *Figure 26* and replace the rest of the values and data labels in the datasheet of *Figure 26* with the data and values of Table 1.

To do so, select **column D** (click on the column head, D, to select the entire column) and then **right-click** the entire selection and navigate down to the **Delete** menu (*Figure 25*).

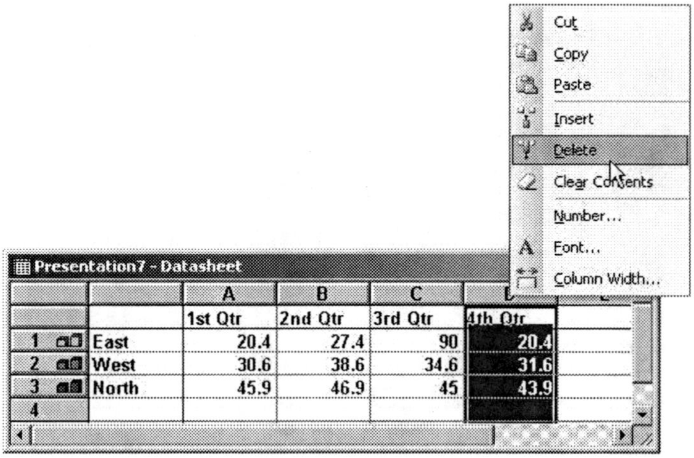

Figure 25

The following screen will appear:

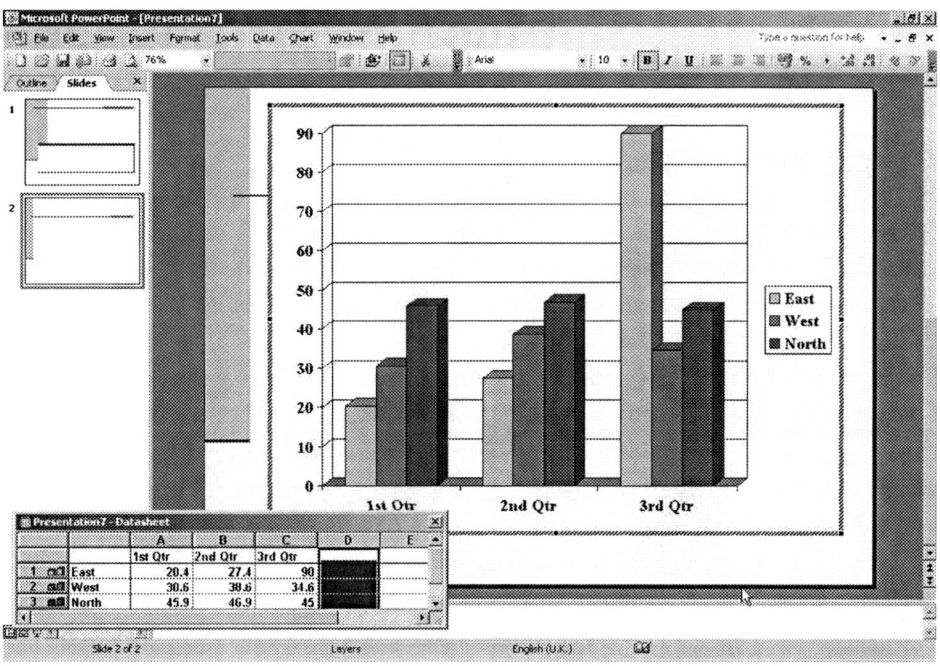

Figure 26

Replace the values and data labels in the datasheet of *Figure 26* with the data and values of Table 1.

A revised diagram is automatically created using the new values and update both the chart and the datasheet (*see Figure 27*).

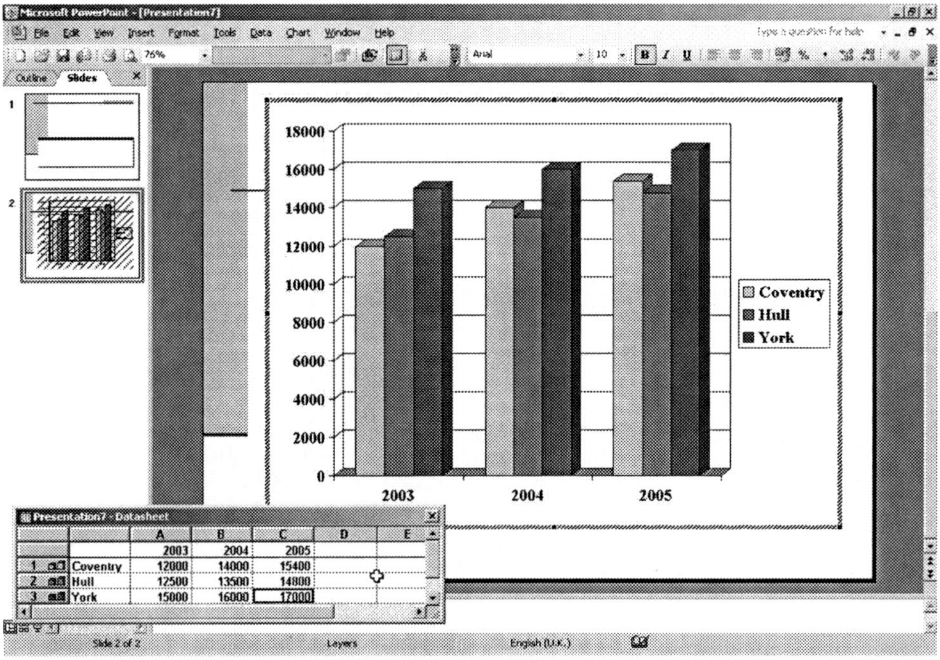

Figure 27

Changing chart types

By default all charts are created in a 3D clustered column format. However, it is extremely easy to change the chart type. As mentioned earlier, PowerPoint uses **Microsoft Graph** to create charts which can create charts in a number of alternative formats such as bar charts, pie charts, line charts, XY (scatter) charts, doughnut charts, radar charts, etc.

To change the chart type, double-click the chart. To change the 3D clustered chart type in *Figure 29* into a line chart, we will carry out the following steps.

Click on the chart to select it, then from the menu bar select **Chart**, and then select the **Chart Type** menu item (*see Figure 28*). The **Chart Type** dialog box will open (*see Figure 29*).

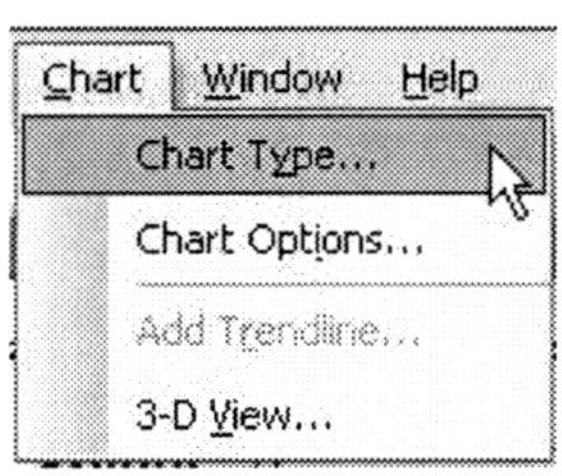

Figure 28

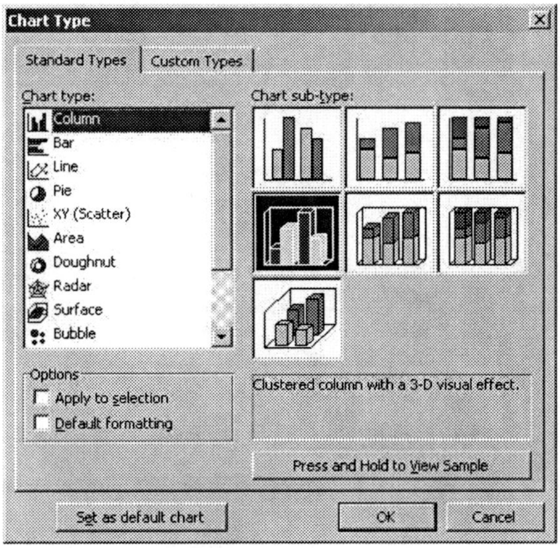

Figure 29

Click on the desired chart type that you wish to apply. Select **OK** to confirm your selection (*see Figure 30*).

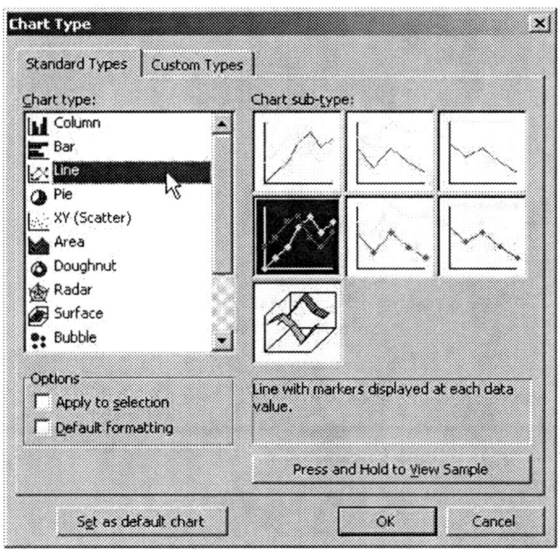

Figure 30

Our 3D clustered chart type shown in *Figure 27* gets transformed into a line chart (*see Figure 31*).

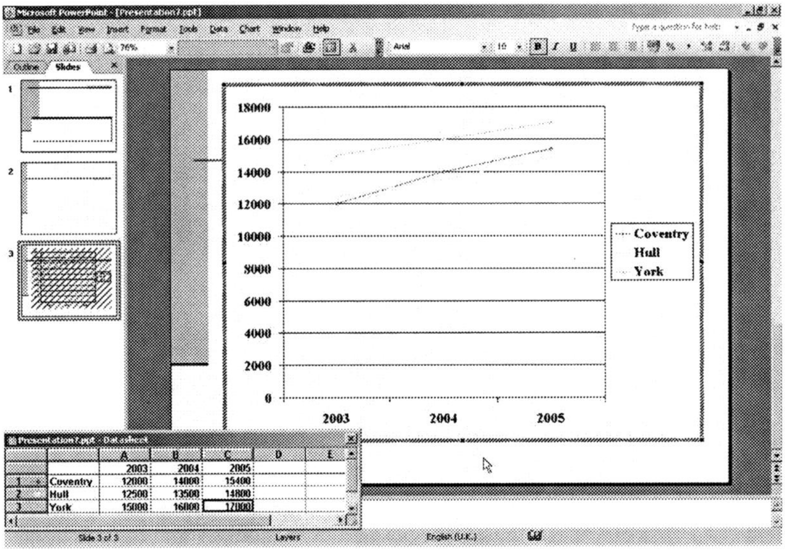

Figure 31

If you are not happy with how your chart looks and would like to return to the original chart type, then select **Edit** from the **menu bar,** and then select the **Undo Edit Object** menu item (*see Figure 32*).

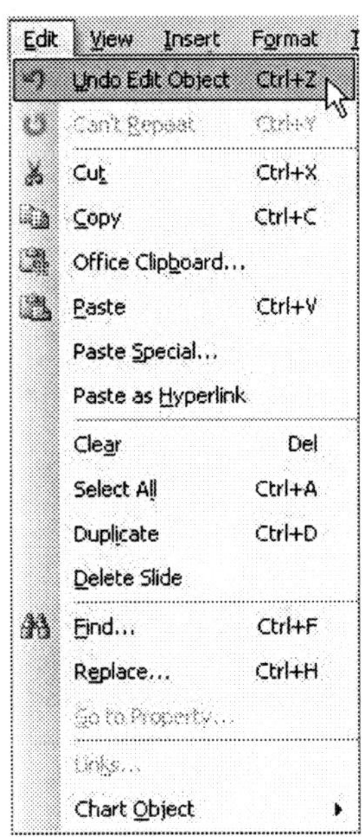

Figure 32

Another way of changing the **Chart type** is to double-click the chart to activate Microsoft Graph and then right-click anywhere in the chart area, but not on the legend or axis, and select **Chart Type** from the pop-up menu (*see Figure 33*).

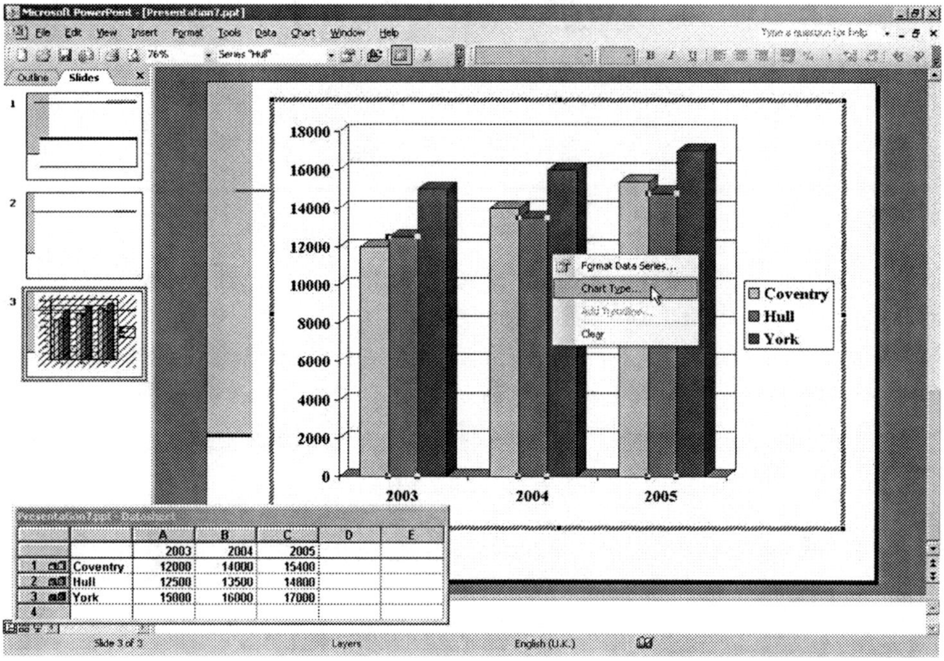

Figure 33

The **Chart Type** dialog box will then open (*see Figure 29*).

Inserting a table

To insert a table in an existing PowerPoint presentation, insert a new slide (*see Figure 19*). From the **menu bar**, select **Insert**, and then the **Table** menu item (*see Figure 34*).

Figure 34

The **Insert Table** dialog box is then displayed:

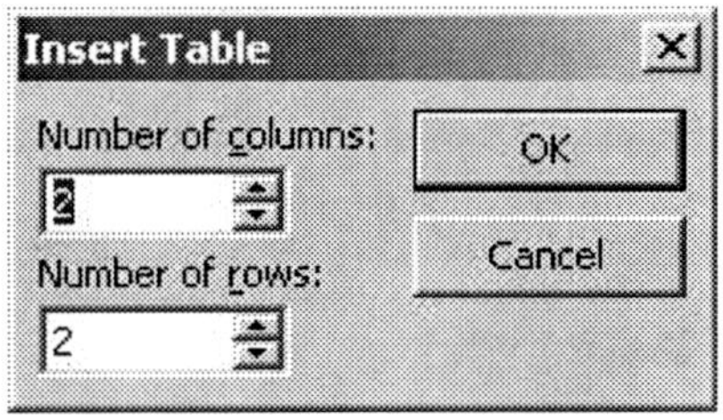

Figure 35

In the dialog box, **Type** the number of rows and columns you want your table to have and click the **OK** button.

In the above example (*see Figure 35*), we are going to create a table of two rows and two columns. (*See Figure 36*).

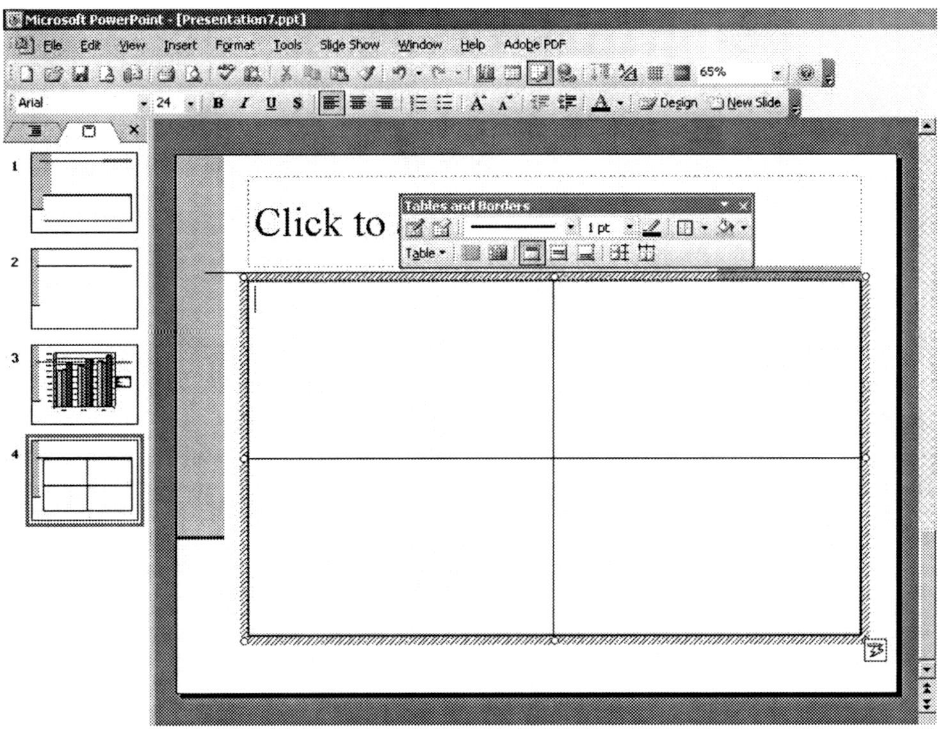

Figure 36

You can now add text to the table by manually clicking in each cell.

Deleting a table

To remove a table from your presentation, simply **click** on the table border (this will select the entire table), and then **press** the **Delete key** on your keyboard. The entire table will be deleted. Use this with caution.

Adding a movie file to a presentation

PowerPoint supports most popular video file formats, such as Audio Video Interleaved (AVI), Moving Pictures Experts Group (MPEG), etc.

To add a movie clip to an existing slide or a new slide from the **Standard** toolbar, select the **Insert** menu, then select **Movies and Sounds**, and finally click on **Movie from File** (*see Figure 37*).

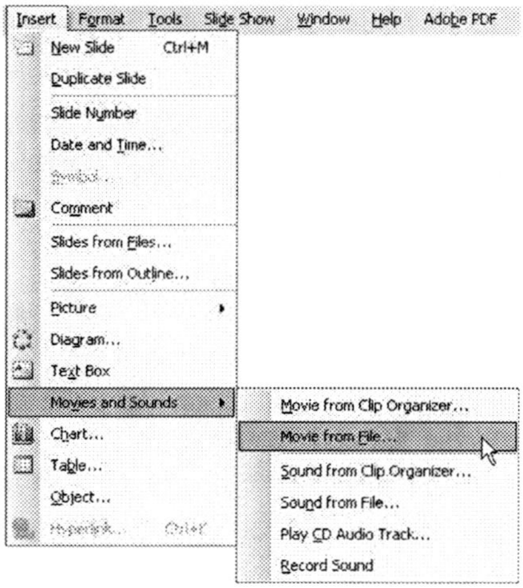

Figure 37

The **Insert Movie** dialog box will appear.

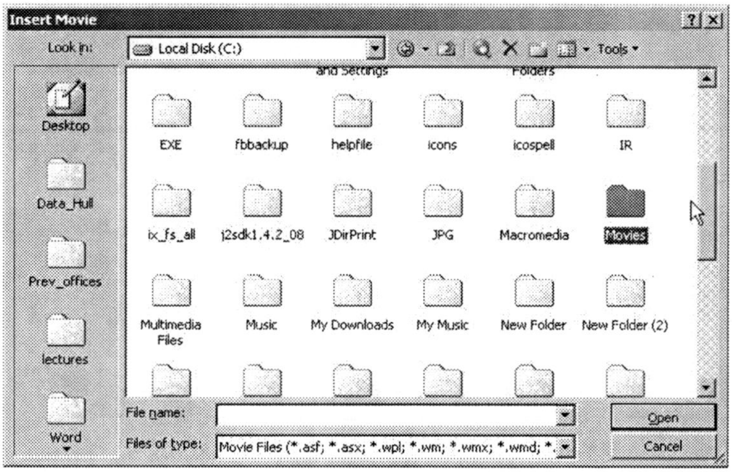

Figure 38

Navigate to the folder where your movie files are located and **select** the movie file you want to insert in your presentation. In our example, all movie clips have been stored on a folder entitled Movies (*see Figure 39*).

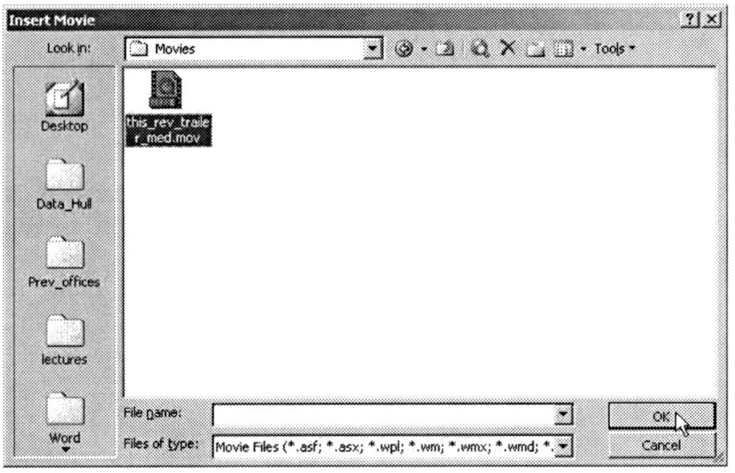

Figure 39

As soon as you click on **OK** in *Figure 39*, your video file will be inserted in your presentation. A dialog box will appear (*see Figure 40*) giving you two choices on how The video file can be played. You can select **Automatically** to have the clip play automatically when the slide is displayed in your presentation or if you want to play the clip manually you should select **When Clicked**.

Figure 40

Setting up the presentation

When all the slides in the presentation have been finalised, you have to decide on the presentation format (there are three types of presentation format).

Each presentation format is appropriate for a particular mechanism of delivery. To view these three options from the **menu bar**, select **Slide Show** menu, and then the **Set Up Show** ménu item (*see Figure 41*).

Figure 41

The **Set Up Show** dialog box screen will be displayed:

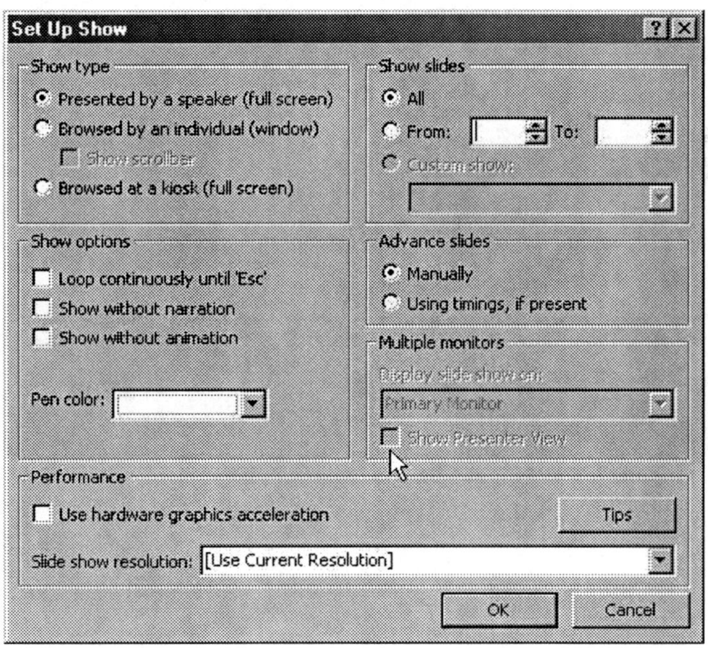

Figure 42

The **Set Up Show** dialog box will allow you to select one of the following three presentation formats:

- **Presented by a speaker (full screen):** This is by far the most common method of delivering a PowerPoint presentation. A full screen, via an electronic OHP system, is displayed for the audience (*see Figure 43*).
- **Browsed by an individual (window):** This method allows others to view your presentation at a time convenient to them. Support is also offered by providing the viewer a browser window with PowerPoint navigation elements such as a scrollbar (*see Figure 44*).
- **Browsed at a kiosk (full screen):** This method enables you to convert your presentation into a self-running full-screen presentation, that loops continuously (i.e. after the end of your presentation it starts over again and this process goes on till you stop the presentation). This type of presentation is generally done for trade shows and exhibitions. The display of this format will be the same as *Figure 46*. An example of the settings for this format can be seen in *Figure 45*.

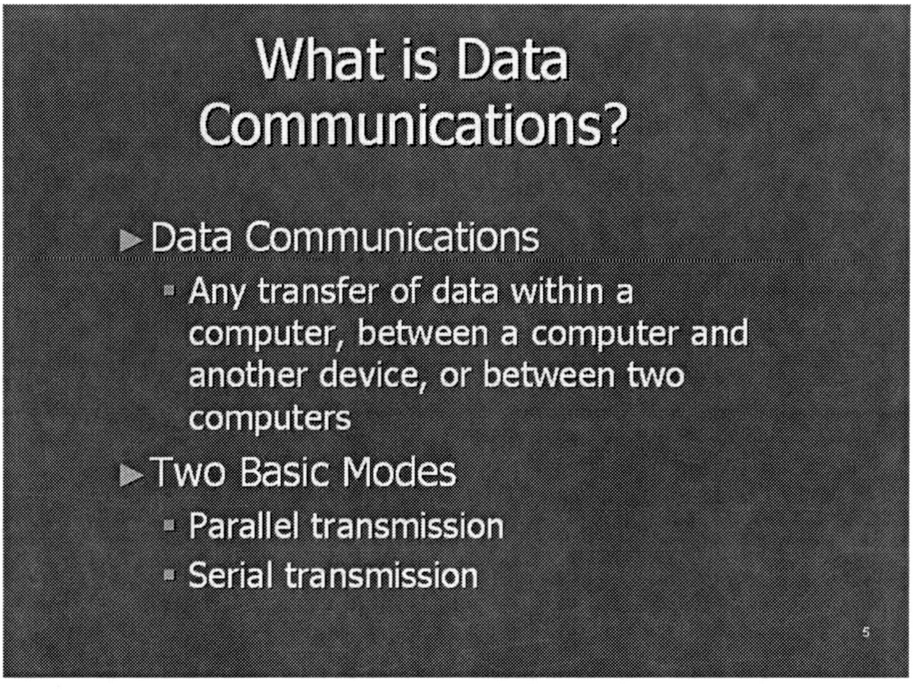

Figure 43

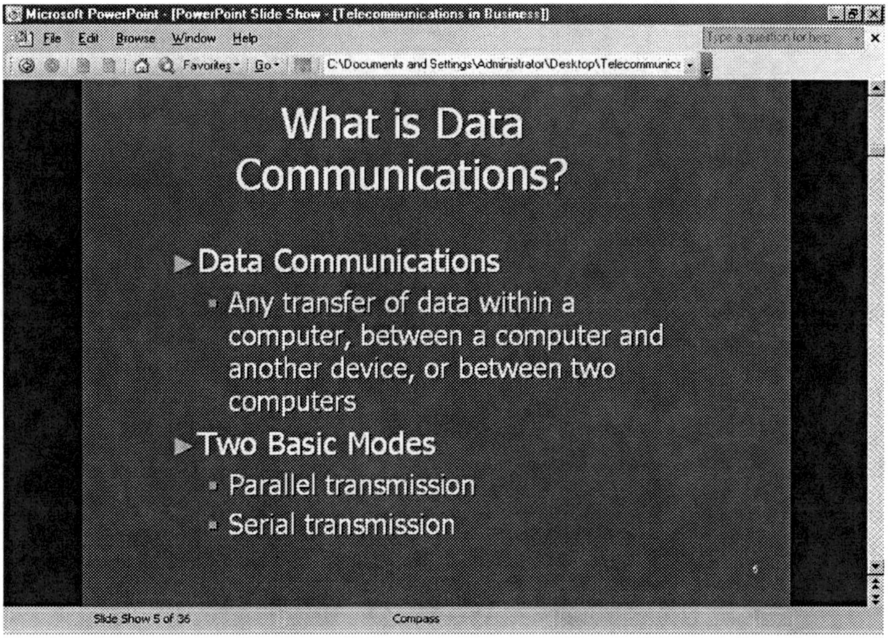

Figure 44

By default, all slides are included when presenting the slideshow (as shown in *Figure 45*). However, it is possible to specify a range of slides to play (i.e. loop). Other options include removal of all animations and narrations (i.e. audio inputs), both of which were selected in the example shown in *Figure 45*.

Another option relates to the advancement of the slideshow (i.e. movement from one slide to another slide). It is possible to advance the slides either manually or using predetermined timings (the latter was selected in the example shown in *Figure 45*).

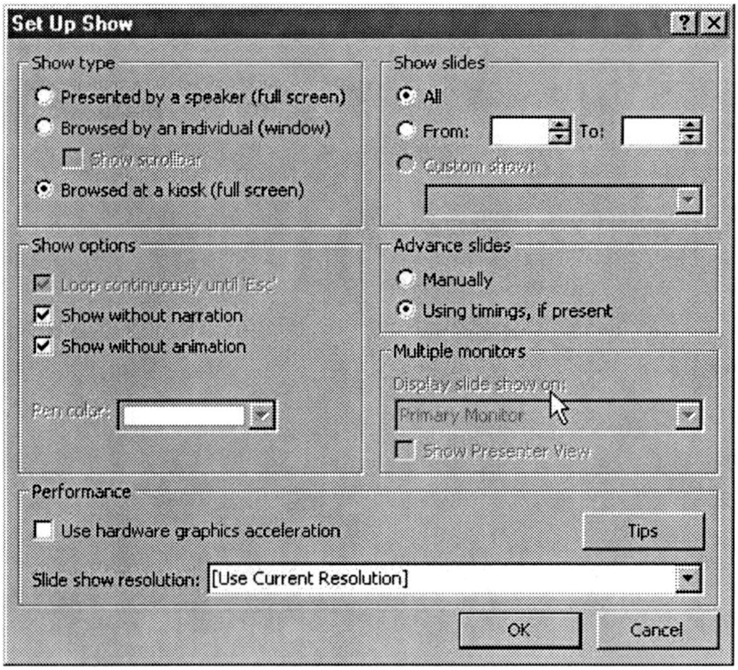

Figure 45

Running the presentation

To run your presentation, open it and click the first slide in the presentation (*see Figure 46*).

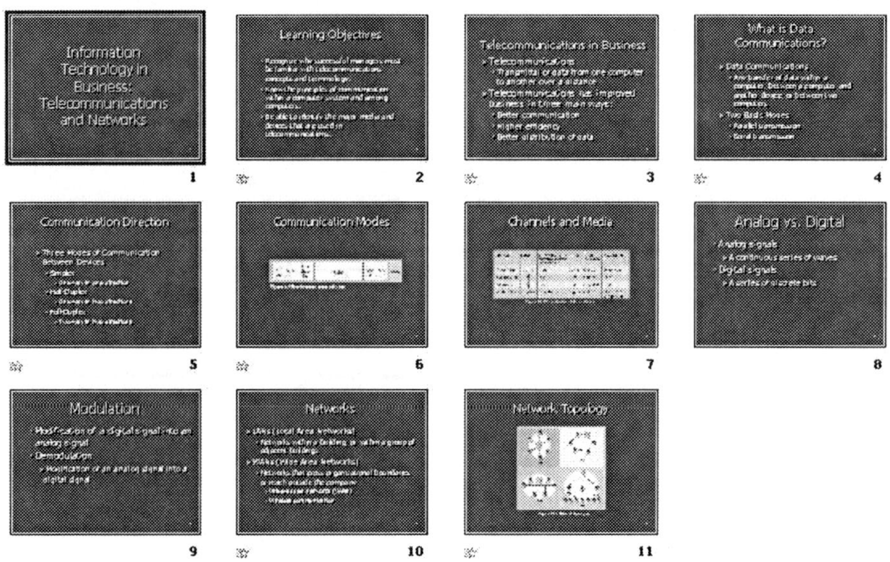

Figure 46

From the **Standard toolbar**, Select **Slideshow**, then **View Show** (see *Figure 47*). The first slide is automatically run in the presentation format mode that was selected (see *Figure 42*). An alternative to this process is to press **F5** on your keyboard.

Figure 47

Index

Q

R

S

T

V

Printed in the United Kingdom
by Lightning Source UK Ltd.
133272UK00001B/152/A

9 781904 995173